THE ARCHITECTURE OF
RALPH ADAMS CRAM
AND HIS OFFICE

ETHAN ANTHONY

W. W. NORTON & COMPANY
New York • London

PHOTO CREDITS

Page 8: Painting of Cram's Portrait. Artist unknown. Photo: Peter A. Juley & Son. (HDB/Cram & Ferguson Archive)

Page 40: Conventual Church of St. Mary and St. John, Cambridge, MA. Photo: Haskell. (HDB/Cram & Ferguson Archive)

Page 140: Rice Institute, Lovett Hall. Photo: Mike Ortega. (HDB/Cram & Ferguson Archive)

Page 200: Watkins Residence, Winona, Minnesota. (HDB/Cram & Ferguson Archive)

For information about permission to reproduce selections from this book, write to Permissions, W. W. Norton & Company, Inc., 500 Fifth Avenue, New York, NY 10110.

Manufacturing by Friesens
Book design by Gilda Hannah
Production manager: Leeann Graham

Library of Congress Cataloging-in-Publication Data

Anthony, Ethan.
    The architecture of Ralph Adams Cram and his office / Ethan Anthony.
      p. cm.
    Includes bibliographical references and index.
    ISBN-13: 978-0-393-73104-0 (hardcover)
    ISBN-10: 0-393-73104-9 (hardcover)
    1. Cram, Ralph Adams, 1863-1942--Criticism and interpretation.
2. Gothic revival (Architecture)--United States. I. Cram, Ralph Adams,
1863-1942. II. Title.
    NA737.C7A58 2007
    720.92--dc22   2006102225

ISBN 13: 978-0-393-73104-0
ISBN 10: 0-393-73104-9

W. W. Norton & Company, Inc., 500 Fifth Avenue, New York, NY 10110
www.wwnorton.com

W. W. Norton & Company Ltd., Castle House, 75/76 Wells Street, London W1T 3QT

0 9 8 7 6 5 4 3 2 1

Contents

Preface and Acknowledgments

My introduction to Ralph Adams Cram began in 1991 when I joined the successor firm to what began as Cram & Wentworth, then called Hoyle, Doran and Berry, Inc., in Boston, Massachusetts. Arriving at the depth of a real-estate recession, I was excited to find that the firm had work and that David Hulihan, the principal, wanted a partner. Though I had heard of Cram, it was primarily due to the clerihew of poet David McCord mocking the funeral urns perched on the roof of the New England Life Insurance building in Boston (see page 238), which my mother had repeated to me.

I had been educated in the tradition, if that is an appropriate word for it, of Le Corbusier and the modernists at the Boston Architectural College, a school that grew out of the Boston Architectural Club, started by Cram in 1889. The dean of the Center, Arcangelo Cascieri, was a sculptor who had worked on a number of Cram buildings, yet I never knew until years later that he also worked with Johannes Kirchmeyer, one of the most important contributors to Cram's interiors.

When I arrived in January 1991, Hoyle, Doran and Berry was hanging on in a basement office space on a corner near Copley Square, the scene of one of Cram's early victories. The secretary, Ann Downs, was over ninety and had been working at the firm since the 1920s. The day I brought a computer in and placed it on her desk she quit: she said she was too old to learn how to use it.

Replacing the drafting tables and parallel rules with CAD elicited a similar response from a pair of octogenarian draftsmen who were still there. Indeed, to keep the firm alive in the modern world it was necessary to update it. At the same time, I began to study the firm archives of photographs and drawings, which soon convinced me that there was something worth saving.

As it turned out it was the spirit that I wanted to save. It was not a question of the people or even the tools but of the work. After World War II, the church commissions that had been the mainstay of the company for over sixty years dried up, and from the 1960s to the 1970s the momentum Cram had established began to dissipate. The last two principals, Austin Cribben and Nisso Aladjem, sold their interest in the firm to long-time project architect David Hulihan in 1988; he was left with the difficult task of trying to save it out of a sense of responsibility to the clients who remained the source of repeat business. But the firm had lost the essential spirit that was the source of its original success; it had become just another firm, albeit one with an interesting history.

My task, as I saw it, was to save the firm from becoming history by recommitting it to the original ideals and principles that had made it great. With this practical starting point I began fifteen years ago. What happened was entirely unexpected, though in hindsight it is completely understandable. I began to like the work I saw and I began to want to design in the same modes and styles. And that is exactly what has come to pass.

In the process of doing the research for this book, it occurred to me that this was a story that had not been told. If I could spend five years in architectural school in Boston and never hear of someone who had been one of America's most renowned architects, why should more distant practitioners know his work? But I found that Cram had been a pervasive influence on generations of students in Boston and that his ideas had spread and were a fundamental part of buildings and institutions in many far-flung parts of the country, if not the world. The story was all around me in bits and pieces.

The book is organized in five parts: a biographical introduction, sections covering selected religious and academic work, a section on residential, institutional, and miscellaneous projects, and a list of the firm's work during the fifty years of Cram's life. All are organized roughly chronologically.

Assembling the project list has meant culling data from many sources including the firm's extensive card files and project lists, and has required extensive verification. Dates are based on the date of the award of projects as the information was kept by the office. The task was complicated because a former principal, now deceased, discarded some of the firm's job books during a move. When sources conflicted, I chose the most reliable dates and attempted to confirm them with other sources.

Unattributed quotes in the text are from Cram's autobiography, My Life in Architecture (Boston: Little Brown & Company, 1936). This well-written work stands today as the best source for information on Cram's life and work.

Acknowledgments
The present manuscript is the result of many years of research that has required the assistance of hundreds of people to follow up and verify in archives, drawings, photographs, books, magazine and journal articles, buildings, ruins, memories, doctoral theses, church bulletins, and anecdotes in the files of the firm and of institutions housed in Cram's buildings. I consulted Cram's letters and those of his family; librarians and archivists; historical societies; rectors and pastors of churches, Cram aficionados, Cram's family, the family of partners and employees over 115 years of office history.

Special thanks are due to Karen

Shafts, librarian in the Prints Department of the Boston Public Library, who supported me during the first two years I spent in the archives with great good humor; David Scudder, Cram's grandson, and Elizabeth Crichton, his granddaughter, who encouraged me and provided me with insights into family life, allowing me to rummage in the remains of his personal library in his daughter's sugar house in Vermont.

Rectors, deacons, archivists, vestrymen, presbyters, and members of Cram's churches have been friendly and helpful beyond the call of duty, especially the Reverend Randall Chase, who encouraged me in the early stages; Rev. Lewis Stone, my friend and rector of All Saints Parish, Peterborough, New Hampshire; and Rev. George Wickersham, canon of the Cathedral of St John the Divine and protector of the Cram legacy at the Cathedral until his death in 2000, who encouraged me to continue the work of the firm and to preserve its history.

I am deeply indebted to those who actively kept Cram's memory alive while his reputation was in the shadows: Austin Cribben, past principal of Hoyle, Doran and Berry, who provided many valuable materials he saved during his fifty years with the firm, and David Hulihan, partner and friend, who saved much that would otherwise have been lost forever during his nearly forty years there.

Among the biographers, thesis writers, researchers, and chroniclers are Robert Muccigrosso, who spent much time with John T. Doran and other principals of the firm. He researched and organized primary source information, some of which is now lost, that he ultimately published in his doctoral thesis. I have not quoted his work specifically but have relied especially on his chronicle of Cram's early years. Without his work my task would have been far more difficult.

Another researcher with access to firm records, who was given a special status by the office from the 1970s through 1984, is Douglass Shand-Tucci of the

Boston Public Library. He enjoyed a privileged relationship with John T. Doran, who sought his assistance in preserving the Cram archives. Author of *Ralph Adams Cram, American Medievalist*, and *Boston Bohemia*, Shand-Tucci advanced the theory that Cram and many of his associates were closeted gays and that much of their artistic endeavor was devoted to covert expression of their sexual preference. I have found no evidence to support his theories.

I am grateful to Ann Miner Daniel, whose doctoral thesis on Cram at the University of North Carolina at Chapel Hill was extremely helpful because it contains primary material based on interviews with key persons who are no longer living.

Cram's work at Princeton was ably chronicled in an excellent paper by Stephen Warnecke of Princeton University. Professor Clara Bargellini's work at the Universidad Nacional de Mexico on Goodhue's Spanish Colonial architecture has contributed much to my understanding of what at first seemed a side track.

Other important works that have provided important background are Richard Oliver's biography, *Bertram Grosvenor Goodhue* (New York: Architectural History Foundation, 1983) and *The Almighty Wall* (New York: Architectural History Foundation, 1983), a biography of Henry Vaughan by William Morgan, who has become a friend and encouraging correspondent in recent years.

Those who have helped me over the years by reading, typing, cataloguing, organizing, and gathering bits of evidence, photographs, and old files include my distant cousin from Virginia, Sarah Bradford, who came to me for a summer after graduating from Sweet Briar and stayed for more than four years working on the book and helping me to keep the firm alive as well. I was able to hire her thanks to a small grant from Annie Ray Watkin Strange, daughter of William Ward Watkin, Cram's assistant in the Rice University project and later his partner in the Houston office the firm maintained until 1922. She walked into the office one day, offered to help me write, and contributed cash assistance.

Pulling the many disparate threads of the story into a more cohesive whole began with important and insightful early editing by Ellen Howards of Boston, editor of *The Arts Weekly*, who helped me to see the way to a story. Jay Pridmore's painstaking and insightful editing over almost a year helped me find and clarify and distill the central themes of the story, and in the home stretch my assistants Meghann Murray and Vanessa Gurshin provided invaluable assistance in editing and retyping endless drafts.

Finally, I thank David Hulihan, Dean James P. Morton of the Cathedral of St. John the Divine, Rev. Lewis Stone, Aileen Laing and Rebecca Lane (formerly of Sweet Briar College), and others who read the manuscript and brought valuable insight to the story.

Special thanks are due to my editor at W. W. Norton, Nancy Green, whose patience and perseverance made this book possible.

1. A Brief Biography

Ralph Adams Cram (1863–1942) practiced architecture during an extraordinary period. He presided over the introduction of Arts and Crafts principles to American architecture, and witnessed the emergence and eclipse of Beaux-Arts classicism and the rise of the International Style of Le Corbusier and Mies van der Rohe. Cram rejected the later strands, finding the soaring, vertical forms of the gothic best suited for articulating his deeply held beliefs about the spirit and function of buildings. Ultimately hailed as the "father of collegiate gothic," Cram is recognized today principally for his campus plans and academic buildings at Princeton and Rice universities and for an extensive portfolio of churches.

The ascendancy of Cram's firm was established with its successful competition entry for the master plan of West Point in 1902. The competition had pitted the firm of Cram, Goodhue & Ferguson, against some of the nation's most famous architects (McKim, Mead & White among them), and the younger firm gained significant recognition as a result. Perhaps equally important, the West Point commission raised neo-Gothic to a prominent position on the national stage.

For Cram, Gothic architecture expressed the fundamental values of spirituality and self-sufficiency with which he had grown up. He believed that architecture was a moral undertaking and that buildings could enrich society and elevate the spirit. His career, like that of his contemporary Frank Lloyd Wright, was a constant search for architectural absolutes. Unlike Wright, Cram found his most emphatically in medieval Europe, embodied in the work of the English Arts and Crafts Movement. Nevertheless he recognized that his clients—largely churchmen and academic administrators—needed functional structures that would keep pace with institutional needs. In this regard Cram was always pleased to note that Gothic architecture was flexible and easily adapted to some contemporary uses. On another level, Cram's Gothic buildings conveyed his spiritual position against industrialization and global war, threats he saw menacing modern society. Ultimately, he was happy to acknowledge that most of his work appealed more to the public than to those who promoted a modern design aesthetic.

In many ways Cram succeeded in reforming what he saw as a decadent society. His religious faith, though not a prerequisite for a church-builder, established a deep connection with many of his clients. Born into a Unitarian family with informal religious precepts, he became an Episcopalian after a religious conversion in Rome and played an integral part in reviving a formal High Church liturgy. Religion overlapped with his interest in the Middle Ages and with what he later called his "Gothic quest."[1] Religion not only informed his architecture; it led him to propose a secular monastic society including the creation of walled towns composed of groups holding similar religious beliefs.

Cram's architecture was also guided by a worldliness that inspired extensive travel, photography, writing, and engagement in literary debate. His writing helped him express and promote the essence of the architecture that he loved, encompassing small churches, ancient priories, and rural manors. Writing bolstered Cram's professional success; in many quarters, he was more widely known for his books and articles than for his works of architecture. In twenty-six books he wrote fiery tracts on various subjects, including society and its moral degradation. He criticized the

I-1. Birthplace and boyhood home of Ralph Adams Cram. Exeter Road, Hampton, New Hampshire. (HDB/Cram & Ferguson Archive, photo: Sarah Bradford 2000)

modernism of the Cubists as egotistical individualism, reasoning that it was a reflection of the general decline of social mores. He was harsher still in his criticism of the generations before Richardsonian Romanesque:

> What followed after 1830 was of very different temper. Jefferson's dilettante passion for "pure Classic" of the Roman mode may have had something to do with the sudden downfall, for, like all amateurs, even those of the High Renaissance, he severed design and style from construction and function. Ionic porticoes, carefully worked out according to Vitruvius, were attached to clapboarded dwellings; Doric columns and entablatures fronted Protestant meeting houses; and, all made of thin boards neatly fitted together, these came for a time the established mode and, as well, a point of departure for a farther and final fall.[2]

Curiously, Cram's buildings were more accepting of contemporary trends than his literary discourse indicates. The architecture of his firm became increasingly eclectic, including Byzantine, Spanish, colonial, and neo-Georgian styles, mirroring the trends embraced by Arts and Crafts designers in Europe. Toward the end of Cram's life, his firm produced art moderne work and a stripped classical building (Cram despised it), but the firm's architecture, even when Cram disapproved of it, never lost touch with the substance of the Gothic.

Cram believed deeply in the power of architecture to educate and influence lives. He called his architecture "organic" architecture, as its design was responsive to the natural environment and to the people who inhabited it. He used the word "vitality" to describe the optimal blend of aesthetic design and functional use. A Goth by heritage (the family name before they emigrated from Germany to England in the seventh century was von Cramm) and a vital one, he was ever vigilant against "archaeological design," his mild pejorative for buildings that "try to appear, in detail at least, of some particular time and some special land."[3] His objective was architecture that was neo-Gothic, original in its design and responsive to its purpose.

At its deepest level, Cram's work reveals a rich intellectual process. Practitioners today can see in his career the dialogues between past and present, Gothic and modern, that influenced his work. By the time he died in 1942, this process, particularly the conscious recognition of historical architecture in modern practice, had been forgotten in favor of a machine aesthetic, but today Cram is recognized as a master who had an uncommon understanding of the importance of historical precedent. He merits study for the deft and artistic touch that translated his meditations on history into works of timeless architecture, as well as for his impassioned ideas about contemporary life.

Childhood and Education

Born on December 16, 1863, Ralph Adams Cram was a member of the eighth generation of his family to live in the small coastal town of Hampton Falls, New Hampshire (fig. I-1). His upbringing was both pastoral, in that it was tied to the family farm, and intellectually active, as the Cram family interests ranged from theology to languages, philosophy, and amateur theatricals.

Cram's Unitarian ancestors, and the entire village of Bilsby, England, had arrived in Massachusetts in 1635. There they quickly found themselves at odds with the Puritans. The dissident group followed their minister north when he was exiled, and they founded the town of Exeter in what would become New Hampshire. Within five years, the need to escape the Puritans' expanding influence drove them farther east, to a remote strip of land along the Atlantic coast between Portsmouth, New Hampshire, and York, Maine. This became Hampton Falls, New Hampshire.

Subsequent generations of Crams worked the land, but their thoughts ranged far beyond agriculture. The broad interests they brought from England leavened the rural life they had inherited. Ralph's father, William Augustine Cram, born in 1837 on the Cram farm, attended the prestigious Phillips Academy in nearby Exeter, but financial constraints prevented him from continuing on to Harvard with his classmates. Instead, in late 1862, William married Sarah Blake (1840–1927), a girl from a neighboring farm. They left for Boston, where William attended Everett Edward Hale's Unitarian Seminary; Sarah returned to the family farm a year later to have their first child. He was named Ralph Adams after Ralph Waldo Emerson and John Adams, two eminent New Englanders of independent character.

In 1866 William A. Cram graduated and was ordained a minister. After a brief stay in Augusta, Maine, he was called to serve a congregation in Westford, near Boston, where the family remained for twelve years, when William returned to Hampton Falls to take over the family farm from his aging father. During the Westford years Ralph and his siblings spent summers and holidays in Hampton Falls with their grandparents. Life on an isolated subsistence farm had made generations of Crams self-reliant and determined, through farming and handcraft, to provide for most material needs as family provided for the intellectual ones. French and German were spoken, and Reverend Cram's library inspired young Ralph. Drawing from this model, the Cram home in Westford became a veritable "intellectual center."[4]

Cram remembered reading Emerson, Kant, Hegel, Spinoza, Matthew Arnold, and John Ruskin before he left home. He was particularly drawn to Ruskin's passionate discourses *The Seven Lamps of Architecture* and *The Stones of Venice*, where he found himself transported to a civilization much older than his own. He was especially captivated by descriptions of Italian churches and Ruskin's concept of them as "vaulted books."[5] Cram's first exposure to architectural drawing was through study of *House Building* (1873) by C. J. Richardson, a gift from his parents on his fifteenth birthday.

Cram's artistic bent was evident at an early age. He had a facility with watercolor and took pleasure in designing and building model towns, constructing the houses, streets, and town squares out of cardboard. At seventeen (fig. I-2), after Cram's graduation from high school in Exeter, his father went to Boston to show his portfolio of architectural drawings to William Ware, founder of the school of architecture at the Massachusetts Institute of Technology. Ware, himself the son of a Unitarian minister, referred the younger Cram to Arthur Rotch, a recent graduate of the Ecole des Beaux-Arts in Paris, who was just then opening a practice in Boston.

Apprenticeship and Travel

For the next five years (1881–86) Cram worked for the firm of Rotch & Tilden as an unpaid apprentice. In spite of the long hours, the imaginative young man took full advantage of the city's cultural

I-2. Ralph Adams Cram at about 17 years of age. (HDB/Cram & Ferguson Archive)

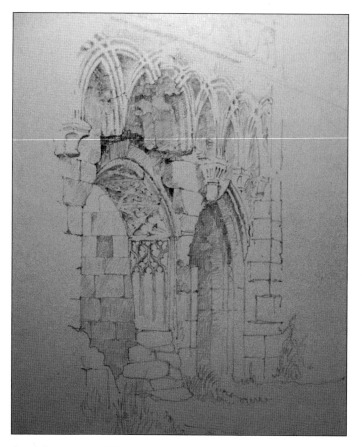

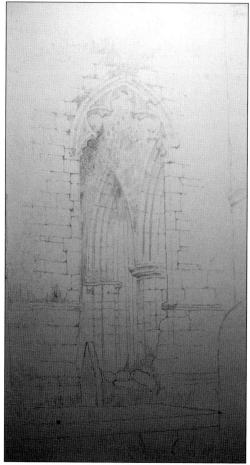

I-3, I-4. Pages from undated Cram sketchbook, c. 1885. (Courtesy of the Boston Public Library–Cram, Goodhue and Ferguson/Cram & Ferguson Collection)

resources. He later wrote of his visits to pre-Raphaelite shows at the Museum of Fine Arts, the first American performance of the operetta *Patience* by Gilbert and Sullivan, and the first American performances of Wagner's operas. He opposed plans for construction of a new apartment building on Copley Square directly in front of Henry Hobson Richardson's monumental Trinity Church; his letter to the editor of the *Boston Evening Transcript* galvanized public opinion against the project, and the plan was withdrawn. Shortly thereafter, a competition was held for the design of a public space. Cram submitted an entry, but the contest was won by his employer, Rotch & Tilden.

Cram continued to seek ways to supplement the meager allowance his father afforded him. Several of his designs for "Small Country Cottages" were published in *The Builder and Wood-worker*, and his letters containing artistic and architectural criticism attracted the attention of E. H. Clement, editor of the *Transcript*, who hired Cram as the paper's art critic. At the age of twenty-two, Ralph Adams Cram had his first paid employment, while he continued to work at Rotch & Tilden and to enter design competitions. His entry for a new courthouse advanced, with nine others, to a semifinal round, but the competition was aborted by city corruption. The semifinalists were paid five hundred dollars each and dismissed, and the commission was awarded to the city architect.

Understandably, Cram was disillusioned, but the money allowed him to leave Rotch & Tilden and embark on his first European tour, a necessary rite of passage for architects of his generation and a long-time dream. The young man arranged with Clement to send back a series of articles about his travels for the newspaper and embarked on a steamship bound for Liverpool, England. On arriving in London, he learned that H. H. Richardson had died, an event he noted soberly as the end of an era.

Cram spent the first several weeks in London and its environs. This was his first taste of European culture and the beginning of a lifelong enchantment with it. He was drawn especially to the ruins of the abbeys that had been the center of medieval life. He eagerly absorbed their rich architectonic language and filled his sketchbooks with atmospheric drawings of the ruins. He took particular pleasure in drawing architectural details. Fragments rise ghostly from the mist in his sketches (figs. I-3 and I-4). Cram next traveled to Paris and to Chartres, where his growing fascination with medieval religious architecture was confirmed. Then he continued to Italy and finally to Bayreuth for the Wagner Festival.

Cram returned to Boston after three months, deeply influenced by European culture and history but without immediate career prospects. He had resigned his position with Rotch & Tilden and lost his editorial job in a dispute with Clement over a negative review—one too many—of an exhibition at a gallery that had advertised in the *Transcript*. Cram was unrepentant, later, in describing the misunderstanding: "After hurling quixotic defiance at the ever courteous and reasonable editor, I descended the long stairs to Washington Street literally without a job. I had forsaken architecture, journalism had cast me out and there was no place for me to go." Of that period, he wrote, "I eked out a precarious existence by doing various odd jobs: designing wallpapers for the friendly George K. Birge of Buffalo, writing and illustrating articles for the *Decorator and Furnisher*—most awful things they were" (fig. I-5).[6]

A second trip to Italy as the tutor to the son of a friend brought Cram in contact with T. Henry Randall (fig. I-6), a young American architect who had recently left the office of H. H. Richardson. Cram and Randall became friends as they investigated ruins by day and haunted medieval churches at night. Whenever Cram could escape tutoring,

I-5. "Jewelers Shop," designed by Cram c. 1885 after leaving Rotch & Tilden. Later Cram disparaged interiors like this. (HDB/Cram & Ferguson Archive)

he and Randall, sketchpads in hand, made careful drawings of the mosaics and floor patterns of Italy's older churches (fig. I-7).

Cram later noted that Randall exhibited a true "passion for good architecture," and this friendship may have helped Cram to rebuild his regard for the profession. Through the friendship, too, his spiritual awareness evolved. His religious upbringing had involved "respectful deism," and he later wrote that it was a restrained Christianity unadorned by art or architecture. Randall, on the other hand, was "vitalized by Catholic tendencies"[7] and invited Cram to attend Christmas Eve Mass in Rome. The event inspired Cram to embrace the formal Catholic liturgy.

A short time later, Cram's employer agreed to release him from his tutoring position, and Cram and Randall seized the opportunity to visit Sicily. Neither knew Palermo outside literary descrip-

I-6. T. Henry Randall. (Photo from *My Life in Architecture*)

I-7. Sketch from San Lorenzo Fiore Church, Rome, c. 1888. (Boston Public Library Ralph Adams Cram Archive)

tion, but they were entranced by the report of two American naval officers they met who claimed that the island was a paradise for anyone interested in mosaics. "Here was indeed a new thing in architecture," Cram wrote. "Roman columns, pointed arches, Byzantine mosaics, Arab inlays of marble and colored glass, Renaissance altars and tombs, all knit together in a perfectly harmonious and organic synthesis."[8] Sicily extinguished whatever vestige of interest Cram might have had in the formalistic compositional training of the École des Beaux-Arts. From Sicily the two friends went to Venice, which exhibited an even more complex array of Moorish, Byzantine, Romanesque, and other influences, but at the same time possessed a certain artistic unity. Of St. Mark's Cathedral Cram wrote that he was amazed by the transcendent eclecti-

cism of the architecture—"all sorts of things assembled and crystallized into a sort of apocalyptic unity in diversity."[9]

Cram returned to Boston newly inspired and determined to establish himself as an architect. He entered the competition for an addition to Charles Bulfinch's Massachusetts State House, a project for which he won second place and a prize of $1,300 (fig. I-8). The award came at a good time; he was without savings and $1,000 in debt to his father. Some members of the political establishment offered to have his entry chosen if he shared some of the profits of the commission with them, but Cram declined, although he considered the addition that resulted such a disservice to the public that he later wondered if his ethical position had been naive.

Eager to open his own practice but lacking the financial resources to do so, Cram began to search for a partner. Fortuitously, a clerk in an art supply store referred him to Charles Francis Wentworth. A draftsman in another firm, Wentworth, like Cram, wanted to go out on his own. The two soon met and began to plan to open an office.

Cram recognized that the death of Richardson opened the field to the possibility of new creative ideas. In 1888, Cram & Wentworth entered a public competition for the Episcopal Cathedral of St. John the Divine in New York City. Neither was selected, and Cram later called his ornate Gothic entry "conscientiously archaeological," meaning, in his lexicon, imitative and without originality.[10] Twenty-five years later Cram would step in as architect of St. John the Divine, by then a beleaguered and incomplete commission, and the result would be regarded as his creative masterpiece.

Cram also initiated an endeavor of a more personal nature. His experiences with Randall in Rome still fresh in his mind, he visited the church of St. John the Evangelist in Boston and put himself in the hands of Father Arthur Crayshaw Hall, an Anglo-Catholic priest of the

Society of St. John the Evangelist, also known as the Cowley Fathers. Cram had determined that the high liturgy of the Cowley Fathers suited him, and he was confirmed by Bishop Brent in the Anglican Communion of the Catholic Church. His spiritual transformation was complete and, by appearances, was strongly connected to the new vigor with which he threw himself into his work.

Cram & Wentworth

In 1889 Cram and Wentworth (fig. I-9) opened their first office, at 1 Park Square (fig. I-10), where they hung a sign, "Cram & Wentworth, Architects."[11] The partnership was a significant step forward, even though the promised commissions dissolved shortly after the firm was established.

In 1889, Cram & Wentworth received its first architectural commission. The firm was asked to prepare preliminary sketches for houses for three retired naval officers. Although these designs were not built, the fees enabled the two young men to move forward with their plans.

Cram & Wentworth's earliest completed work was a house built in 1890 in Brookline for Lee Hammond, a Boston liquor dealer. Next came a commission to restore an apartment house in the suburb of Allston, and Wentworth was commissioned to design an addition to a church in Brattleboro, Vermont.

New opportunities now came from many different directions. In 1890 Wentworth married and settled with his wife in the streetcar suburb of Brookline. Shortly thereafter came a much-needed commission for a summerhouse in York Harbor, Maine, from Wentworth's mother-in-law, Marion Whittemore. Referrals from family and occasional loans from Wentworth's uncle Howard were indispensable in keeping the partnership going in the first, difficult years. Wentworth's membership in the Church of Our Savior brought him into contact with William Lawrence, later

I-8. Competition entry, watercolor, for the Massachusetts State House addition, 1887. (HDB/Cram & Ferguson Archive)

the Episcopal bishop of Massachusetts, who probably gave them useful contacts.

In slack periods, of which there were many, the partners entered competitions for churches, often with disappointing results. Their proposal for St. John's Williamstown (fig. I-11), a church with a large summer congregation from Boston, was rejected after investment of considerable time and effort. The commission was awarded to William Ware, but the client, Benjamin Ide, compensated them with a commission to design a town house for him.

An office history noted that Cram & Wentworth had entered the competition for a new cathedral for Dallas, Texas, and it may have been that unsuccessful entry that brought Bertram Grosvenor Goodhue, the New York architect who won, to the notice of the young Boston firm (fig. I-12). Just twenty-one and working for James Renwick Jr. in New York, Goodhue needed an office where he could find the support he required to complete the drawings for the Dallas Cathedral. It is not known why he chose to travel to Boston, where he proposed to carry out the project

I-9. Charles Francis Wentworth. (Photo from *My Life in Architecture*)

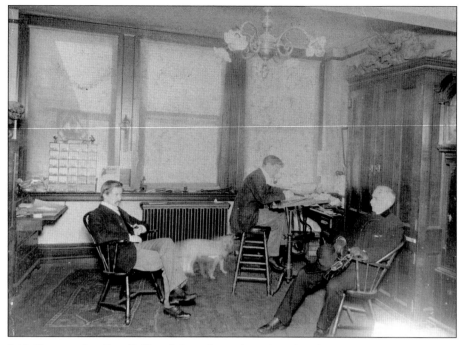

I-10. Bertram Goodhue (left) and Cram (center) work with a client, assisted by "Jack" the dog, in one of the earliest Cram & Wentworth office photos. One Park Square, Boston. Date unknown. (HDB/Cram & Ferguson Archive)

I-11. Watercolor by Cram of proposal for St. John's Church, Williamstown, Massachusetts. (HDB/Cram & Ferguson Archive; photo: Richard Creek)

Goodhue was exceptionally well suited to the small firm. His family background and upbringing closely paralleled that of Cram. He had been born and raised in Pomfret, Connecticut, a town founded when six men, including John Grosvenor, an ancestor of his mother, purchased land from Native Americans in the late seventeenth century. His father, Charles Wells Goodhue, had deep roots in New England as well: he was descended from one of the original settlers of Brattleboro, Vermont. Like Cram, Goodhue demonstrated early artistic talent, but his family favored a more practical education, sending him to a military boarding school in New Haven. At fifteen, he packed up his drawings and headed to New York, where he became an apprentice at the Renwick firm.

Cram and Goodhue were sympathetic and highly complementary as architects. Massing, proportion, and composition were Cram's strengths, while detail of the most exquisite conception was Goodhue's. "From a professional point of view he was my alter ego," Cram wrote.[13] Goodhue was masterful at designing and rendering details ranging from buttress-like mullions to liturgical furniture. Unattached to what Cram called "Christian culture," Goodhue "saw the problem from a purely aesthetic point of view, and this vivid imagination led him to think of all he did as adventure, invention, the exploration of new fields."[14] Cram rarely followed Goodhue's lead, preferring to pursue English and French Gothic models while his younger partner explored the Spanish colonial and baroque.

From the beginning, the relationship was not without rough spots. The first was caused by the failure of the Dallas cathedral authorities to pay their bills. The church elders demanded a series of redesigns in an effort to reduce costs and adamantly refused to pay Goodhue until they were satisfied. Ultimately, the cathedral authorities abandoned the project altogether, which placed considerable stress on Goodhue's relationship with his

jointly with Cram and Wentworth, but as Cram noted, "He was promptly taken on as one of our first draftsmen."[12] This suited Goodhue, who resigned from the Renwick office on October 10, 1890, and moved to Boston.

new colleagues. Wentworth again borrowed money from his family to keep the firm going and wrote to Cram that "Goodhue will have to go."[15] However, Goodhue eventually did bring in new work, notably a project from his cousin, General Charles H. Grosvenor, for a memorial gateway arch for the Confederate Cemetery at Chickamauga Battleground in Chattanooga, Tennessee (fig. I-13). The arch was never built, but the architects presumably were paid.

In 1891, Cram & Wentworth received a commission for three houses in Aspinwall Hill (see page 203), a development in Brookline planned by Frederick Law Olmsted. The subdivision, named for developer William Aspinwall, president of the Panama Railroad, incorporated curving streets that preserved the existing contours of the landscape. This approach was a departure from conventional clear-cut wooded areas and streets and lots laid out in a rectilinear grid. Inspired by the terrain of Aspinwall Hill, Cram designed the houses in what he called "English half-timber" style, with gables and half-timbered upper stories inspired by the work of the British Arts and Crafts Movement architect Richard Norman Shaw (1831–1912), first introduced to New England by architect Henry Vaughan (1846–1917) (fig. I-14) with his 1882 design for St. Andrew's in Newcastle, Maine. Vaughn was an Englishman who had become a powerful influence on East Coast architects as a result of several influential commissions. Before emigrating from England, he had worked in the office of George Frederick Bodley, an eminent architect of the Gothic revival. In America, Vaughn first worked for Richardson, but he soon established a practice that ran substantially counter to the heavy arches and rusticated bases of the Richardsonian vocabulary.

Cram's Brookline houses, though conventional, appeared fresh in design and settled into the landscape—in the terminology of the time, they were organic.

But building houses did not provide a living. Cram & Wentworth needed a direction for their practice. Cram told Wentworth that he was interested in "a comparatively virgin field," he recalled; he noted that "a careful study indicated that there was such a field, and that was one for which my new interests, acquired in Rome, argued acceptance."[16] This was the building of churches.

Drawing on the ideas of Ruskin and the Oxford movement, Cram believed that Gothic architecture could be revived and new, entirely original churches built with an architectonic vocabulary drawn from the Middle Ages. The Oxford movement was a revitalization of the English Catholic Church following the Catholic Emancipation Act of 1827. Its most visible proponent was A. W. N. Pugin (1812–1852), designer of the

I-12. Bertram Goodhue, c. 1910. (Photo from *My Life in Architecture*)

I-13. Ink drawing by Bertram Goodhue, one of several schemes for Chickamauga Arch, Chattanooga, Tennessee, in an unusual classical style, 1897. (HDB/Cram & Ferguson Archive)

I-14. Henry Vaughn, c. 1905. (Photo from *My Life in Architecture*)

I-15. Rendering by Roger Hayward of the Chapel of Saints Peter and Paul at St. Paul's School, Concord, New Hampshire, 1888. The original building by Henry Vaughn is at left; the 1927, Cram addition at right. (HDB/Cram & Ferguson Archive)

Houses of Parliament and advocate of the first Gothic revival. Through Pugin and Ruskin the arts-and-crafts movement flowered, and inspired many architects of the time to move beyond Richardsonian Romanesque. The preference for Gothic form was reinforced by the Oxford movement's belief that religious architecture must reflect its liturgy. Cram's reading of Ruskin and Pugin probably introduced him to this idea, and its corollary, that non-Gothic architecture represented non-Christian or "pagan" origins. Vaughn's Gothic-inspired chapels, including those at St. Paul's School in Concord, New Hampshire (fig. I-15), shown here with a later Cram addition), and Groton School in Massachusetts, became inspiring examples for many architects with traditional tastes.

Within a few years, Vaughan, like Richard Norman Shaw, moved on to Georgian architecture and eventually was forgotten. Cram & Wentworth inherited the mantle of "the most esteemed Gothic practitioner" in America.[17]

In the early phase of their careers, and with freedom to follow their muse, Cram and Wentworth designed "suppositi-tious" churches and submitted them to magazines. These unbuilt projects were almost entirely Gothic, following, Cram noted, "the precedent established by John D. Sedding, at that time the most vital and inspiring of contemporary English ecclesiastical architects."[18]

In 1891, the firm was invited to submit a design for the new church of All Saints Parish in Ashmont, Massachusetts, outside Boston (fig. I-16). Consisting of Cram's rugged massing richly illustrated by Goodhue's lively drawings, their proposal was accepted and the resulting church—a strong monumental building—was hailed as a great success. Many elements of the church referred to the English Gothic that Cram had studied and photographed. The crenellated tower quoted from examples at Magdalen College, Oxford, a feature that reappears in later Cram designs. The composition bears out his view that Gothic churches could be original. The seam-cut granite was economical in Boston and distinctive in the realm of the Gothic revival. So was Cram's restraint and exclusion of detail or "absurd archaisms," as the critic Claude Bragdon wrote a few years later.[19] Bragdon was sufficiently impressed to compare All Saints to the powerful unity that characterized the skyscrapers of Louis Sullivan.

Even before completion of the church, All Saints captivated potential clients who saw drawings of it. Suddenly, the firm's reputation soared, and it quickly acquired four more substantial church projects in the Boston area: St. Paul's in Brockton (fig. I-17), the Swedenborgian Church in Newtonville, Christ Church in Hyde Park, and All Saints in Brookline (fig. I-18). In all, Cram's touch, primarily his powerful massing, are in evidence. They were not as striking at All Saints Ashmont, but they were prominent and distinctive, and they expanded a portfolio that was soon to place the firm among Boston's leading church architects.

This initial good fortune did not last:

business was already in a state of contraction when the stock market crashed in 1893, and the situation became dark for most architectural firms. In that climate, the firm was fortunate to win an invited competition for the Second Congregational Church (later Phillips Exeter chapel) in Exeter, New Hampshire (fig. I-19).

Their first submission was a colonial scheme that Cram based on his knowledge of the simple Georgian vernacular of southern New Hampshire. Happily for him, after awarding the commission to the firm, the committee changed direction and requested a church in the Gothic style instead. The final design is a powerful composition of rough granite block, revisiting some of the themes Cram had recently explored at All Saints Ashmont, but on a smaller scale and with the powerful added element of a corner tower.

By the time the Exeter church was

I-16. All Saints Church, Ashmont, Massachusetts, 1891–92. The lychgate on the south and the massive tower on the west provide counterpoints to the powerful clerestoried walls of rock face granite. (HDB/Cram & Ferguson Archive: photo: Paul J. Weber)

I-17. Cram, Wentworth, and Goodhue's early scheme for St. Paul's Brockton shows Goodhue's influence in the vertical buttresses framing the west door. (HDB/Cram & Ferguson Archive, office reprint from *American Architect and Building News*, October 8, 1892)

THE TOWER AND CLOISTER CLOSE.

I-18. Rendering of All Saints, Brookline, Massachusetts, by Bertram Goodhue in a tour-de-force of pencil entourage. Undated drawing for a fundraising booklet published by the church. (HDB/Cram & Ferguson Archive)

completed, the economic depression was in full swing. The partners occupied themselves with projects other than buildings. Goodhue published his first book, *Mexican Memories*, based on his recent travels by rail through Mexico and his observations of Spanish colonial architecture. Cram designed heraldic seals for a number of institutions, including Sweet Briar College, Wheaton College, and the dioceses of St. Louis and Chicago. He also pubished his "little indiscretion," as he later called it: *Black Spirits and White* was a collection of stories of the supernatural that drew heavily on his European travels for scenic backgrounds.[20] Goodhue designed the book and the typeface for it.

Cram, Wentworth & Goodhue

In 1895 Wentworth, ill with tuberculosis, went to California. Work was scarce; the partners did not wish to lose a valuable ally and decided to offer Goodhue a partnership. Although the date of Goodhue's partnership has been debated, according to Cram's autobiography it was 1895. Cram spent the summer of 1897 in England photographing churches for his first architectural publication, a folio of photographs entitled *English Country Churches* (fig. I-20).

Wentworth died in December 1899, a hard blow for Cram. He and Wentworth had been friends and business partners for nearly a decade, working together closely to lay the foundation for the firm's future. Wentworth had mediated the incipient rivalry the other two "insistent egos," as Cram described himself and Goodhue.[21] Without Wentworth, the competition between the two, light-hearted at times, could turn bitter.

For several years Cram and Goodhue got along well enough, bonded perhaps by the economic straits they faced together. They collaborated on *Church Building*, written by Cram and illustrated by Goodhue (fig. I-21). It was a catalog of church designs, proposing the ideal type for any use or setting, from village and town structures to city churches and cathedrals. Practical in its approach (it distinguishes between "good English design" and "bad stonework" or "unintelligent design,"[22] it was generally eclectic in its taste and became a ready reference for other architects and especially for clients in determining a suitable style for their churches. Cram was characteristically effusive in the text. "Art is the result of beautiful ideas, of beautiful modes of life, of beautiful environment," he wrote. "He would be a courageous optimist who would say these things exist now in secular life."[23] He averred that the church in America currently "does not stand a higher degree" than secular institutions in artistic expression, but emphasized his conviction that religion provided the best chance to achieve beautiful and inspiring architecture.[24]

Church Building was crucial to the firm's growing reputation. As the book was distributed to the rectors of Episcopal churches throughout New England, it became a kind of primer for pastors to learn the basics of church design. Simultaneously, completed designs such as All Saints in Ashmont, Christ Church in Hyde Park, and All Saints in Brookline were published in magazines and journals. With this professional endorsement, the office of Ralph Adams Cram and Bertram Grosvenor Goodhue was becoming the logical choice for any congregation seeking to build a church of high visibility and prestige.

Marriage and Family

Before the turn of the century, Cram had achieved a measure of the success that he had imagined he might someday enjoy. His good fortune was not solely professional. On September 20, 1900, in New Bedford, Massachusetts, he married Elizabeth Carrington Read, a woman of beauty and commanding presence. Bess came from a prominent Richmond, Virginia, family that had moved north after the Civil War (fig. I-22). Over the years, the Reads would provide valuable southern connections that brought new business to the firm.

The Crams' honeymoon repeated in broad outline the itinerary that Cram had followed on his first European tour. Bess too was moved by the soaring profiles of English Gothic churches and shared Cram's preference for the English Perpendicular (fig. I-23). It is likely that the trip sparked her own interest in liturgical vestments and altar cloths, an aspect of church design in which she became expert. This was the first of many European trips the couple took together to explore the source of Cram's artistic imagination, to hunt for articles to adorn his churches, and to find craftsmen who Cram would eventually bring to Boston.

Upon their return the couple settled briefly in Richmond Court, a new apart-

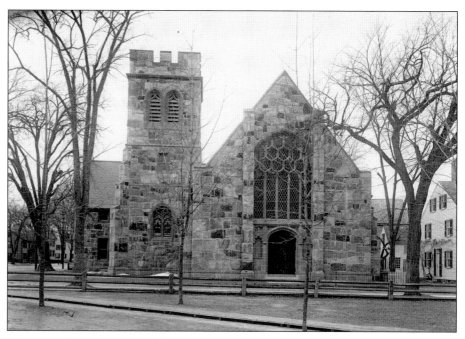

I-19. Second Congregational Church (later Phillips Church), Phillips Exeter Academy, Exeter, New Hampshire, 1895, showing Cram's penchant for rock-face granite. (HDB/Cram & Ferguson Archive, office reprint from *American Architect and Building News,* March 15, 1902)

I-20. St. Mary the Great, Cambridge, England: it closely resembles All Saints Ashmont. (From *English Country Churches,* Boston, 1898)

ment complex in Brookline designed by the firm in Elizabethan style, based on Hampton Court Palace (fig. I-24). Soon the Crams' finances permitted them to move to a fashionable town house on Beacon Hill in Boston. A daughter, Mary Carrington, was born on Novem-

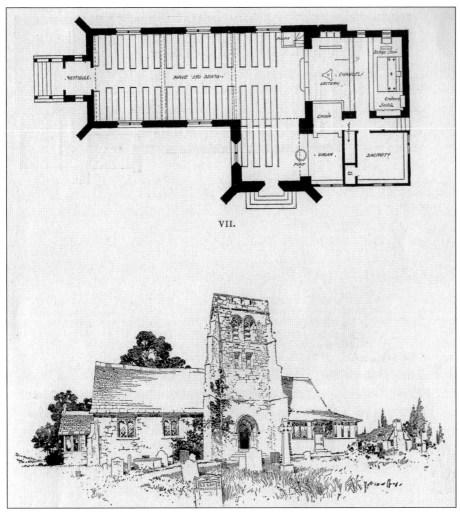

VII.

I-21. Cram's design, rendered by Goodhue, of a proposed church, showing Cram's debt to English country churches: the design is based on the church at Bramber. (HDB/Cram & Ferguson Archive)

The partners rang in the new century confident that their prospects were bright, though they were frequently disappointed that the road sometimes seemed slow. The situation changed suddenly in a manner, as Cram liked to remember, that was partially fortuitous. As he later wrote:

> Returning at the end of the year [1900], I took up once more the not very promising affairs of the office. And then as though signaling the end of one epoch in my life and the beginning of another of wider scope, something happened that changed the whole current of our history. Going one morning to the office at 53 State Street I opened up the limited amount of mail that lay on my desk. There was one long and unpromising envelope that bore the earmarks of an advertisement and I started to throw it, unopened, in the wastebasket, for I disliked advertising then as much as I do now. On second thought I opened it. It was a formal notice from Government officials that we had been invited to take part, with nine other firms, in a competition for the rebuilding of the United States Military Academy at West Point, at an estimated cost of some seven million dollars.[25]

Cram was quick to understand the politics that accompanied the awarding of a commission on this scale. Cram, Goodhue & Ferguson had been invited specifically to represent the Gothic style used for some of the campus buildings and which a group at the Academy believed should set the tone for new buildings at West Point.

Also competing was the powerful New York firm of McKim, Mead & White, well known for neoclassical Beaux-Arts design. While some campus buildings were in the Gothic revival style, McKim, Mead & White had recently completed Cullum Hall on the campus. Thus, the competition was designed not just to select an architect,

ber 19, 1902 and a son, Ralph Wentworth, on September 18, 1905. A third child, Elizabeth Strudwick, was born at Whitehall, their country house in Sudbury, on August 29, 1913 (fig. I-25).

Cram, Goodhue & Ferguson

By 1900, Cram, Wentworth & Goodhue was showing modest growth. In 1901, the partnership expanded to include Frank Ferguson, who had joined the firm as engineer in 1891. Ferguson had acquired great skill in applying modern construction techniques, such as wrought-iron trusses, to the firm's historical styles. At the same time, Frank Cleveland and Chester Godfrey, both natives of Hampton Falls, joined the firm as draftsmen. All three men would but also to determine the stylistic direction for the campus as a whole.

The jury included, among others, Cass Gilbert of New York, known for his Gothic urban designs, most notably the Woolworth Building in Manhattan. Cram accurately viewed the competition as a "battle of the styles."[26]

McKim, Mead & White appeared to be the frontrunner, based on the firm's prominence and on the early decision to limit presentation drawings to orthographic, two-dimensional projections, as taught at the École des Beaux-Arts. Cram did not participate in the discussion because mechanical failure on his train from Boston kept him from attending the meeting where the ground rules of the competition were established. Beaux-Arts renderings were McKim, Mead & White's specialty, and the exclusion of the romantic perspectives favored by Gothic-style architects posed a significant handicap for Cram, Goodhue & Ferguson.

However, Cram returned to Boston determined to succeed, telling his colleagues "we might yet win through if our plan was good enough."[27] The firm hired William Wells Bosworth, a skilled draftsman who could render their plans in the best Beaux-Arts fashion. Cram later said that "what he accomplished came very close to making amends for that exclusion of perspective which, in the beginning, had seemed to us would be fatal in the result."[28]

The triumph came one morning in May 1902, when a draftsman in the office placed a copy of the *Boston Herald* on Cram's desk. A front-page story carried the news that the firm had been selected as architects and master planners of the United States Military Academy. The Gothic had prevailed. The firm's design featured "a dependence on mass and composition for our effects," as Cram later described it, and the elimination of "adventitious detail."[29] In a shot at critics who assumed that Goodhue had been key in winning the commission, he said "that detail and ornament

I-22. Gathering of Elizabeth Cram's family at Whitehall, Sudbury, Massachusetts in the mid-1920s. Cram is standing (center left), Bess is standing next to him, and her brother-in-law Edmund Strudwick is seated at her feet. (HDB/Cram & Ferguson Archive)

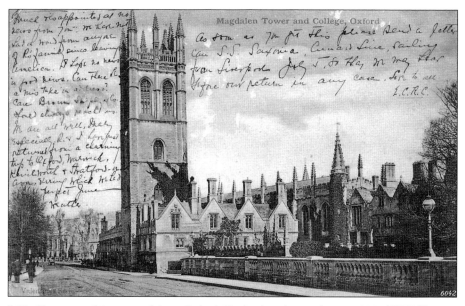

I-23. Cram sent this postcard from Oxford, England, to his mother in 1904. (HDB/Cram & Ferguson Archive)

were a minor factor in architectural design."[30]

Critic Montgomery Schuyler wrote in *Architectural Record* that the Gothic entry "faithfully applied to modern conditions."[31] The architects had demon-

I-24. Richmond Court, Brookline, Massachusetts, c. 1900. (HDB/Cram & Ferguson Archive, reprint from *American Architect & Building News*, October 21, 1899)

I-25. Cram at Whitehall, date unknown. (HDB/Cram & Ferguson Archive)

strated that the spirit of medieval buildings could be evoked in original designs and that old forms could be recombined to suit contemporary purposes. Cram's use of a local stone that blended with the rugged cliffs over the Hudson River and the Gothic scheme were attractive to the

jury on many levels (fig. I-26), which commented, as Schuyler reported, "the character of the design is such that it cannot only be constructed with economy, but that it will harmonize with the character of the landscape, and that it can be readily developed into a satisfactory and complete plan."[32]

While the commission represented a great triumph for Cram and his office, there was a tangle of practical matters to address in executing the work. The firm moved to larger quarters at 15 Beacon Street and opened a second office in New York, as required by the competition. Contractual arrangements and fee negotiations were complicated by politics. "We are warned that, intentionally or not, the relations of the government with architects had usually resulted either in breaking their hearts or their bank accounts," Cram later wrote with the benefit of hindsight.[33] Whatever the financial difficulties, the commission raised Cram, Goodhue & Ferguson to a new level of importance among East Coast architectural firms (figs. I-27, I-28).

More important, the West Point commission provided Cram, Goodhue, & Ferguson with the opportunity that they had been seeking: to create an architectural iconography drawn from history and apply it to a modern institutional program. Cram designed for the Post Headquarters building a profile that resembled Mont St. Michel in Normandy, one of Europe's most famous Gothic images. The Post Headquarters' impregnable ramparts and crenellated towers express an unmistakable military image (see page 151).

If there was any controversy, it was focused on Goodhue's design for the Cadet Chapel. Distinctly English, it was criticized by a vocal minority. This criticism was silenced when the completed chapel was overwhelmingly lauded for its indisputable beauty. The firm's overall plan for the Academy accomplished everything that could have been expected of it. It was intended to inspire, as Cram himself later explained, a sense of rootedness and nobility in the nation's officer corps. It was, and still is, the psychological home of the United States Army. Cram had succeeded in branding the military.

In 1904, with Goodhue managing the West Point project from New York, Cram returned to England to study and photograph ruined abbeys, revisiting the architecture that had impressed him so strongly on his previous trips. This time, the expedition resulted in a book that he characterized as a pilgrimage to certain holy places, *The Ruined Abbeys of Great Britain*. Cram's homage to the monastic movement and the life of faithful contemplation, the book recounted the story of the suppression of the monasteries in the fifteenth century as part of the English Reformation, the event that ended the Gothic period in religious architecture. The buildings that remained were in many cases little more than empty shells, but Cram used them as models to inform his own work. *Ruined Abbeys* was historical commentary that provided the philosophical basis for work to come. Cram lamented the end of the monastic way of life and attributed many later social ills to the reformation. "To the monks England owes her conversion and to them in large measure her civilization," Cram wrote. "For a thousand years monasticism flourished within her borders. . . . in five years the material fabric was annihilated, but its memory remains, and will endure forever: this alone persecution was powerless to destroy."[34]

Cram's ambition was to revive monastic architecture as a means of resuscitating the moral foundations of society. The massing and organization of English abbeys in his work became stronger than ever, particularly in his campus plans, where he was clearly inspired by the abbeys' blending of religious and educational purpose. He incorporated cloisters as connecting elements between buildings. Tower entries, great halls, and medieval en-suite circulation also became characteristic elements of the firm's

I-26. Post Headquarters, United States Military Academy, West Point, New York, date unknown. (HDB/Cram & Ferguson Archive; photo: Paul J. Weber)

I-27. Photo of the Cram, Goodhue, and Ferguson firm office, undated, Boston. (HDB/Cram & Ferguson Archive)

I-28. Office Christmas party photo, undated, probably taken by Cram, who enjoyed photography. The man standing at left, with mustache, is Chester Godfrey; William Ward Watkin is second from right. (HDB/Cram & Ferguson Archive)

academic architecture. The broad adoption of these forms by other educational institutions affirms that Cram was at least successful in memorializing monastic architecture, if he did not succeed in reintroducing a monastic mentality.

A church closely modeled on the English monasteries is the 1905 Unitarian Church of West Newton, Massachusetts. Here Cram used the tower and the cloister as organizing elements, providing access to the quiet inner cloister garth, or yard, through the bell tower. The concept of a spiritually focused inner precinct protected from the bustle of an urban setting became a model for many of the firm's churches.

The medieval theme was extended into the interior at West Newton Unitarian. Cram employed the extraordinary talent of Johannes Kirchmeyer, an artisan born in Oberammergau, Germany, to execute the lavish interior carving. With Cram's help, Kirchmeyer had emigrated to New York in 1880 and soon found his way to Boston, where Cram provided financing for a studio and gave him multiple commissions. (Kirchmeyer also found work with Henry Vaughan on the chapel at St. Paul's School and a chapel for the sisters

of St. Margaret's on Beacon Hill). Cram described Kirchmeyer as a "true creative artist, for while he was possessed by the whole Mediaeval tradition, he was bent on working this out in vital contemporary forms."[35] Kirchmeyer himself sometimes attributed his more elongated, modern-looking work to something akin to the American skyscraper. Whatever the inspiration, Kirchmeyer's handmade ornament was essential to the overall Gothic feel of Cram's churches.

The firm's involvement in larger, more complex projects required organizational changes in the office. Cram reflected on this evolution in a letter to his mother. "Success is like a battle, once on the firing line there is no backing out while the flag is on the captured rampart of the enemy . . . ," he wrote. "It is a great game for one born active and sanguine, a fierce joy but sometimes I wish there was a monastic order that took in married men and their families. Now and then I get a little tired of responsibility."[36]

Younger architects joining the office were sharing the responsibilities of a larger practice. In 1905, with Goodhue in Manhattan, Frank Ferguson and Frank Cleveland began to take a more active role in Boston. In July 1906 Raymond Hood joined the New York office, where he worked for a year before being fired by Goodhue. In 1908 Alexander Hoyle joined the office. New projects were distributed to Boston or New York depending upon the source of the commission and the location of the work. Draftsmen circulated between the two offices, and ideas were exchanged. Since all engineering was supervised by Ferguson in Boston and all detailing by Goodhue in New York, neither office could operate autonomously. Together Ferguson and Cram could achieved often-breathtaking Gothic interiors with large spans and sleek profiles that were also more typical of modern construction than the medieval.

During the initial period of separate offices, the latent rivalry between Cram and Goodhue manifested itself in informal competition, friendly at first, perhaps even stimulated by team spirit, office versus office, over the design for Calvary Church in Pittsburgh. Cram and Goodhue agreed that each office would submit its own proposal and let the client choose (figs. I-29, I-30). Cram won, and, for reasons certainly unrelated to his besting of Goodhue, was deeply proud of this church. "The best thing we ever did or shall do," he put it in a letter to his wife.[37] Most likely he was referring to the fact that Calvary was based faithfully on Whitby Abbey.

In 1907 the competition became decidedly less friendly when the firm was invited to compete for the commission of St. Thomas Church in New York to replace a building destroyed by fire (fig. I-31). Goodhue was preoccupied with West Point, so Cram designed the submission, which was rendered in the New York office (Goodhue provided the interior details and decoration). When the design won, Cram revised the original scheme to include a French flamboyant aspect, which Goodhue disparaged. Goodhue tried to change the elements of the scheme; Cram was livid. He called New York to complain. An emotional argument ensued, with Ferguson joining Cram. Neither side held back from criticizing the designs of the other. Goodhue was deeply offended, but he proposed that the client should see both schemes, without the designers' names. Again Cram's was chosen, and, although Goodhue apparently accepted the decision, the conflict created a barrier between the two that ultimately could not be overcome.

Publicity about West Point continued to bring in other prestigious academic commissions. In 1907 Woodrow Wilson, then president of Princeton University, appointed Cram consulting architect for the campus. Wilson's objective was to resolve the architectural cacophony of the buildings and to encourage an identification of Princeton with the traditions of the medieval university, specifically Oxford.

As campus planner and the designer of four buildings, Cram could now explore the relationship between education and religious life. He imagined the Graduate College as a cloistered community. Here he could apply his ideas about religion as the means to moral regeneration on an undeniably important canvas. In 1910 the university awarded him an honorary doctorate of letters for his work.

The Graduate College at Princeton is one of Cram's academic masterpieces

ACCEPTED DESIGN FOR CALVARY CHURCH, PITTSBURG, PA.   CRAM, GOODHUE & FERGUSON, ARCHITECTS

MAIN FLOOR PLAN.

ALTERNATIVE SCHEME "B."

I-29. Winning design for Calvary Church, Pittsburgh: the Boston office's design rendered in an undated watercolor by Cram. The design is simple and massive. The Parish House tower recalls the Nashua library. (HDB/Cram & Ferguson Archive, office reprint from *Architectural Review*, undated)

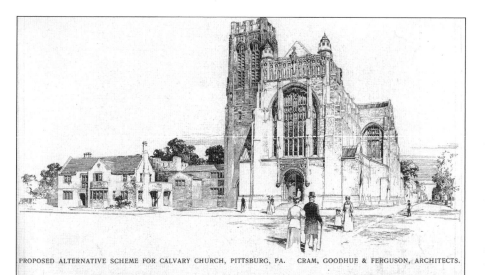

PROPOSED ALTERNATIVE SCHEME FOR CALVARY CHURCH, PITTSBURG, PA.   CRAM, GOODHUE & FERGUSON, ARCHITECTS.

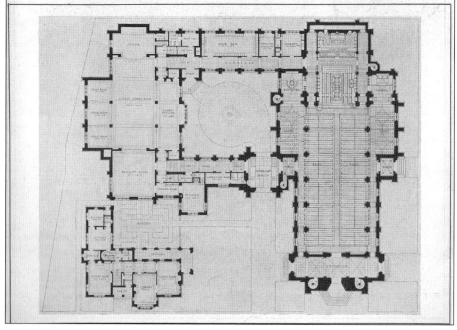

I-30. Design for Calvary: the New York office's design in an undated rendering by Bertram Goodhue. Far more detailed, no raw spires, Goodhue's mini-buttresses at the west entry recall West Point. The Parish House is far more residential and spread out. (HDB/Cram & Ferguson Archive, office reprint of *Architectural Review*, undated)

materials is no reason why we should throw away stone, and oak, and carving, and metal work, and stained glass."[38]

Despite the controversy, the work of Cram, Goodhue & Ferguson at Princeton clearly appealed to the academic establishment. It led to the commission for a master plan and first phase of buildings at Rice Institute in Houston in 1908; Edgar Lovett, president of the new school, had been a member of the Princeton faculty. But the Rice campus took a new direction—what Henry-Russell Hitchcock later termed a "Byzantoid" turn.[39] Cram at first suggested that a Spanish colonial style would properly reflect the Hispanic heritage of the area. Rice trustees rejected this approach, primarily because of fresh memories of the Mexican War of 1846–48.[40] As an alternative, Cram proposed an original Byzantine-Romanesque style employed for more than a dozen buildings on the campus and followed even today by Rice.[41]

A chance encounter on a transAtlantic crossing in the company of Bishop David Hummel Greer of New York in 1910 brought Cram, Goodhue & Ferguson a second opportunity to work on the Cathedral of St. John the Divine in New York. Ever since the competition had been awarded to Heins & La Farge in 1892, the project had been fraught with obstacles. Site conditions required much deeper excavations than anticipated to support their massive Romanesque design; the longer it took to make any progress at all in construction, the more the design was challenged. Cram was one of a number of architects who published critiques of the project and suggested remedies. The situation was further complicated by the death of George Heins in 1907 and the appointment of William Messer Grosvenor as the new dean of the cathedral in 1910.

Though the causality was consistently denied by Cram, not long after his journey the trustees of St. John the Divine rejected further work in the Romanesque style and endorsed Cram's

(fig. I-32). Like West Point, it too expressed the debate between tradition and modernism. As the modernist cry grew loud, if not yet particularly widespread, against the Graduate College, Cram was joined by Goodhue in a clear, if dismissive, response to the contentious moderns and their arguments. "Steel framing and reinforced concrete are good enough in their way when used as the servants of the architect," Goodhue said. "Just because we have such

Gothic plan, in spite of the difficulties such a change would entail. In 1911, the trustees voted to release Christopher Grant La Farge from his contract and hired Cram.

The change in the midst of construction was infuriating to supporters of Heins and LaFarge, and the change had the appearance of high-handed manipulation. The code of ethics of the American Institute of Architects at the time forbade one architect from taking work commissioned to another (it no longer does), and many members of the profession believed, incorrectly, that Cram had committed such a breach. Some friends of La Farge, including Cass Gilbert, a longtime Cram supporter, and a circle of East Coast architects said publicly that it was unthinkable for Cram to accept the commission; Gilbert sent a personal appeal to Cram asking him to decline the job. Goodhue, who sought greater social acceptance in the New York architectural community, was dismayed, yet Cram would not back down. The trustees had acted according to their contract, which stipulated that the firm could be dismissed in the event of the death of either partner. La Farge asked the ethics committee of the AIA to censure Cram. It was a bold move; Cram was not only one of the nation's leading architects, but also a member of the committee. He properly recused himself from the deliberations. In time, the ethics committee exonerated him, and he worked for the next twenty years on the problem of creating a building of Gothic proportions on the partially built Romanesque foundations (figs. I-33, I-34).

St. John the Divine was finally on course architecturally, but considerable resentment lingered, especially among New York architects, and this probably affected Cram's relationship with Goodhue. Goodhue's feelings about the situation were complicated. Publicly, he declared that he opposed accepting the commission because the circumstances reflected badly on the firm. However, Goodhue's biographer Richard Oliver

COMPETITION · S · THOMAS'S · CHVRCH · NEW · YORK ·
FRONT · ELEVATION ·

I-31. Original competition submission for St. Thomas Church by Cram, Goodhue, and Ferguson, c. 1907. (HDB/Cram & Ferguson Archive; photo: Richard Creek)

has suggested that he may have felt Cram's involvement and the controversy would threaten his own acceptance in New York architectural circles. It is also possible that he resented Cram's working on the cathedral design himself rather than referring it to the New York office.[42] In any case, after several threats of resig-

I-32. Graduate College, Princeton University. Princeton, New Jersey, date unknown. (HDB/Cram & Ferguson Archive; photo: Howard Cox)

nation, in 1913 Goodhue withdrew from the partnership, perhaps encouraged to take the step by the knowledge that he would soon receive the commission to design St. Bartholomew's Church on Park Avenue.

Cram and Goodhue thus finally completed their separation, which had begun ten years earlier with the winning of the West Point commission. Cram remained in Boston, changing the firm name to Cram & Ferguson. While emotionally wrenching, the break was arranged so that each could continue ongoing work without disruption. Cram retained the West Point and St. Thomas Church commissions. Goodhue kept the New York office space and a commission for the Panama–California Exposition in San Diego. The two men did not meet again for eight years, but Cram was always generous in his assessments of his former partner. In 1936 he wrote, "Goodhue never swerved from his vital originality, working always further and further from archaeology and precedent, while I suppose I represented the reactionary tendency toward these very precedents he could use so superbly as his

point of departure, as his spring-board, from which he launched himself into that fine adventure which led in the end to such vivid and original conceptions as the Nebraska State Capitol."[43] Goodhue, for his part, wrote Cram that he missed the give-and-take of their friendship and the sounding board they had provided for each other.

Cram & Ferguson

Despite the falloff in work caused by the war in Europe, a few new commissions came to the firm after Goodhue's departure—a Georgian academic building at Phillips Academy in Exeter, New Hampshire in 1914 and two buildings at Wheaton College in Norton, Massachusetts, in 1915 and 1916, all executed largely by Alexander Hoyle (figs.I-35, I-36). Providentially, in 1914, Cram was asked to assume the position of head of the Architecture Department at the Massachusetts Institute of Technology, a title he demanded in order to not seem subordinate to the academic chair.[44] Cram undertook teaching with a measure of ambivalence. He had no academic training in architecture and had expressed the view that architecture schools were elitist and dedicated to turning out narrow specialists. He also noted that MIT, like most other institutions of higher education, did not teach religious architecture. So Cram offered a studio on the design of a church, a course that was enthusiastically received by the students.

Eventually Cram conceived of an improved school of architecture that would be "half college and half monastery."[45] This opinion, he conceded, ran counter to the secular trend of society, but he believed the formation of character was more important than the acquisition of specific knowledge. He further held that the builders of the great cathedrals had no formal education. Cram wrote later that the number of students who chose architecture was growing because the profession was regarded as "fashionable and gentlemanly," but most of his students were not fit to be archi-tects: "My experience led me to believe that about sixty percent of the men in the Department at any time were absolutely unfitted to become architects or even good draftsmen."[46] (Today, the dropout rate in many schools of architec-ture is even greater.)

Cram's position at MIT afforded him a forum to speak out against the narrow formalism of Beaux-Arts training, which consisted of learning the vocabulary and instruction in a fixed set of rules for assembling the elements in a balanced composition. Cram insisted that archi-tecture was a holistic exercise (though he did not use that word), and he required a senior thesis that forced his students to consider history, art, and other disci-plines related to good design.

A highlight of Cram's tenure at MIT was his role as impresario of its Fiftieth Anniversary pageant in 1916, an event that also marked the institution's move from Boston to a new campus in Cam-bridge. In an era when architects were celebrating industrial materials and the exploitation of machines, Cram staged a medieval festival with 1,700 participants costumed in Arthurian garb. Part of the program was a symbolic ferrying of dig-nitaries, including the mayors of Boston and Cambridge and the governor of Massachusetts, in barges across the Charles River. Entitled "The Masque of Power," the event dramatized milestones of Western history on a large stage. Pre-siding over the festivities was Cram him-self as pageant marshal, a role he performed dressed as Merlin the Magi-cian.

By 1914 Cram was a prominent figure in Boston. His affection for the city and concern for its future persuaded him, during the slack war years, to accept an appointment, from the infamous Mayor Curley, as the first chairman of the Boston Planning Board, which he chaired from 1914 to 1922. His enthusi-asm for the bustle and diversity of city life increasingly was displaced by a grow-ing concern that the living conditions in

I-33. First known sketches by Cram for the central tower scheme of the Cathe-dral of St. John the Divine, New York City. Date unknown. (Collection of the author)

I-34. Plan sketches by Cram for central tower scheme of the Cathedral of St. John the Divine, New York City. Date unknown. (Collection of the author)

I-35 and I-36. Administration building, Wheaton College, Norton, Massachusetts, by Alexander Hoyle, 1932, showing the influence of the English Arts and Crafts Movement in the office. The colonial-style interior of the Administration building is typical of many academic buildings designed by Hoyle. (HDB/ Cram & Ferguson Archive; photo: Arthur C. Haskell)

poor areas contributed to the general decline in social values and mores. During his tenure the "sewers and rat holes and general unpleasantness that existed" along the Charles River banks were replaced with the park now known as the Esplanade, scene of summer concerts of the Boston Pops Orchestra.[47]

Cram's most elaborate, even quixotic, effort as a planner came in 1919, when he proposed the construction of St. Botolph's island in the Charles River basin (fig. I-37). Imagined along the lines of the Ile de la Cité in Paris, the complex was to include civic structures such as a new city hall, a cathedral, and an open-air theater. Though Cram's proposal was denounced by those who lived on Beacon Street, whose views would have been impeded, the plan was not without impact. It focused Cram's attention on the fate of American cities in general.

His book *Walled Towns*, written in 1919, was a reaction against industrial city life, drawing on his experience on the planning board and his battles against "modern civilization . . . its fundamental weaknesses were its imperialism, its materialism and its quantitative standard . . ."[48] His solution for modern society, as the title suggested, was a return to small communal villages, such as those of medieval times and also, more practically, to his nostalgic vision of life in the New England countryside.

Although Cram had attained a level of material success beyond that of all but a handful of architects, his writings put him in a unique, perhaps compromised position politically.

In *The Nemesis of Mediocrity* and *The Substance of Gothic*, both published in 1917, he had leveled broad criticism at modern society and especially democracy. The latter book, drawn from a series of lectures he gave at the Lowell Institute, described the medieval period in Europe when society in general was deeply connected to religion. The secular ideas of the Renaissance that followed, he wrote, changed things for the

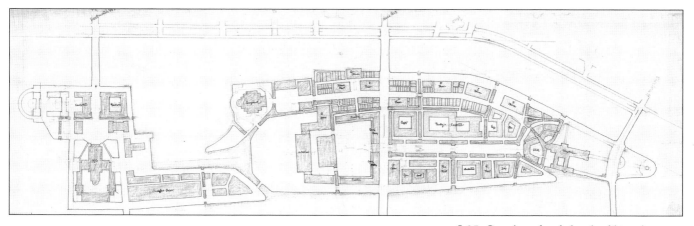

I-37. Cram's undated sketch of his scheme for a cultural and entertainment island in the Charles River, Boston, Massachusetts. At its center was to be a new Episcopal Cathedral. (HDB/Cram & Ferguson Archive)

worse. And with apocalyptic acuity, he predicted that World War I would change things again, "for the blast of war is puring away the dross, and the alchemy of the world's agony is transmuting base metal into refined gold."[49]

The Nemesis of Mediocrity attacked modern society at large. "During the Middle Ages," he wrote, "when the ideal of democracy was at its highest point, and when it was most nearly achieved, it was held as incontrovertible that the purpose of political organization was primarily ethical and moral, and that its function was the achievement of righteousness and justice."[50]

What he mourned were untrammeled growth, imperialism, and the loss of communal life. In his youth Cram had been an avowed socialist, and in his later years he declared his distaste for democracy as a tyranny of the majority. He abhorred international communism and opposed organized labor on the grounds that it was a leadership of the most by the least. He acknowledged that communal experiments, such as those of the Shakers and the Roycrofters, had failed, but he never gave up his hope for radical social transformation.

While Cram was politically torn, he was aesthetically unambiguous. In 1921, elected to Phi Beta Kappa at Harvard, he expressed his views on the subject of art at his induction ceremony:

There is a spirit in times as there is a spirit in men and it is this whereby each lives in spite of the accidents of casual deformity, either of body or of character. It is this inner spirit that reveals itself through art in its many forms. It would appear, therefore, that art is in some curious way an expression not of the personal reactions of highly specialized individuals, but of something that is communal even racial in its nature. I have scant sympathy with that entirely modern view of art that makes the artist a rebel against a constituted society, an abnormal phenomenon, feeding upon his inner self, cut off from the life of his fellows, and issuing his aesthetic manifestos in flaming defiance, and in the conviction of superiority, a being for whom laws are not, an art for which there is no general acceptances for it there need be no conscious and vital link with the art of past generations.[51]

Aged fifty-eight, on the cusp of the most productive year of his career, Cram was aware that certain of his convictions of his were losing popularity. Nevertheless, he used his power and his reputation to advocate with passion for religious faith as the center of a secular academia made suspicious of social institutions by the war. In the final stage of his career, Cram would become increasingly isolated from the architects who sought to promote modernism. But his socially conservative viewpoint resonated with many men who, thanks to the boom of the twenties, had the means to finance major commissions. Among these, St. George's School Chapel in Newport,

Rhode Island, Princeton Chapel, East Liberty Presbyterian Church in Pittsburgh, and his final plan for the Cathedral of St. John the Divine (see pages 115–117) rank as his greatest architectural achievements.

The Final Decades

The character and organization of Cram & Ferguson changed significantly after World War I. In 1925 Cram was honored as *Time* magazine's Man of the Year, an extraordinary recognition for an architect. The firm grew, occasionally reaching a staff of as many as sixty employees. It was not departmentalized like other large firms. Instead, new partners were added to support the creative reach of Cram, who continued to rough out designs but did not follow them through to completion. There were many new projects, and those that had been interrupted by the war were revived. The younger partners of the firm gradually assumed more responsibility. Chester Godfrey had taken over engineering after Ferguson's death in 1925 and added a new marketing responsibility, traveling to visit clients.

Frank Cleveland specialized in Gothic design; Chester Godfrey and Alexander Hoyle in Georgian design (all three were admitted to partnership in 1926).

If anyone in the office could be considered Cram's protégé, it was Frank Cleveland. Hailing, like Cram, from Hampton Falls, Cleveland began as an office boy in 1900, as Cram had begun at Rotch & Tilden. A quiet man with modest social skills, Cleveland adopted the spirit of Cram's Gothicism while bringing a talent like Goodhue's to detailed design and rendering.

The academic portfolio expanded under Alexander Hoyle. Hoyle, a graduate of Concord Massachusetts Public High School, who won a scholarship to Harvard and a fellowship to the American Academy in Rome, joined the firm in 1908. He was thoroughly comfortable with the Georgian vocabulary. He applied it to multiple projects at Phillips Exeter Academy, Wheaton College, and Williams College. John Doran, Cram's youngest assistant, who joined the firm in 1927 (he was admitted to partnership together with Chester A. Brown and William H. Owens in 1944) tended toward the Gothic and contributed heavily to the firm's major work in that style, especially the Cathedral of St. John the Divine.

The firm's work was predominantly Georgian, occasionally Romanesque (for Catholic churches), and Spanish colonial, in the South. By choice Cram was most deeply involved in projects based on English Gothic precedents. But even in the Princeton University Chapel, designed with Alexander Hoyle, English Gothic was interwoven with decidedly French accents, derived from Cram's post–World War I trips to France.

While Cram's admiration for the Gothic only deepened through his life, his interests, if not his personal design repertoire, broadened with visits to Spain, the first journey taken in 1922. It was an architectural epiphany: he found there the sources of Goodhue's Spanish colonial in the original, and he commis-

I-38. Cram's undated watercolor of his design for the Guild steps to Boston Common from Beacon Street, Boston, Massachusetts, bears his monogram. This example demonstrates how Cram's renderings are different from those of Goodhue. (HDB/Cram & Ferguson Archive)

I-39. Julia Idelson wing of the Houston Public Library, Houston, Texas, in an undated photo showing its Mediterranean terracotta roof, Spanish parapet frieze, and Romanesque arches recalling themes of Cram's 1922 trip through Spain. (HDB/Cram & Ferguson Archive; photo: Paul J. Weber)

sioned measured drawings of the roots of the style, at Palma Mallorca Cathedral, and produced a book about it in 1932. As he wrote in *American Architecture* magazine in 1924: "I at last encountered Spain, and since that eventful six months nothing else seems to matter much, not even the little villages of England, the tall cathedrals of France [or] the hill towns of Italy—not even, (and with shame it be spoken!) not even Palermo or Venice or Carcassone."[52] In Spain, the Catholic monastic life had been preserved; the fine medieval architecture had survived without "renovations," and Cram was deeply attracted to it.

With institutional projects like the Houston Public Library (1926) (fig. I-39), and the Doheny Library (1930) at the University of Southern California (fig. I-40), Cram followed the path of the Arts and Crafts Movement to its end high in Venetian Gothic. He elaborated his Venetian with Romanesque ideas, no doubt influenced by excitement generated by Harvard professor John Conant's excavation work on the Romanesque complex at Cluny. This expedition, begun in 1920 and partially supported by a subscription among Boston architects organized by Cram, revealed much of the decorative work at the abbey, and its echoes can be seen in the undercroft of Cram's St. George's Chapel.

Cram saw the Gothic in broader focus now and was eager to say so. In the 1924 edition of *Church Building,* he reiterated the importance of the crusading spirit of architects like himself who sought the redemption of religious art. His underlying purpose had not changed; it had grown stronger. "There is nothing in the early editions the author would retract . . . unless perhaps it were the rather narrow enthusiasm for the latest phase of English Gothic as the sole basis of religious architecture so desired at the time. Apparently one becomes less of a purist, or rather stylist, with advancing years, finding beauty in unexpected places and significance in things once disregarded."[53]

Cram's activity as social critic was increasingly evident. As he finished commissions, including World War I memorials and his great Gothic works of the 1920s, he enjoyed the acclaim that accrued to him at the dedication of these monuments. His speech at the dedication of the Princeton Chapel was an opportunity to expand on his growing realization that religion would no longer be taken for granted; it had to compete for the interest of people:

The formal dedication of the Chapel remains to be the more important task of making this building something more than an architectural factor in the composition of the campus, of weaving it, so to speak, into the very fabric of undergraduate life. We have

I-40. Doheny Library, University of Southern California, Los Angeles, California, date unknown. The massing continues themes Cram first developed at Rice University and in the Houston Library. Where those projects drew on Venetian themes, at Dohery Cram overlaid the massing of the Adrian Gate at Constantinople, which he visited between the Rice and USC projects. The interiors reflect his interest in Spanish medieval architecture. (HDB/Cram & Ferguson Archive; photo: Padilla Studios)

reached a point where, largely, perhaps wholly, through its own fault, religion has ceased to make that universal appeal. Religion has separated itself from flourishing life and is either disregarded or looked on as vieux jeux, an amenity of life, perhaps like art or open plumbing. Princeton Chapel must make its appeal to the free will and compel acceptance by the strength of its dynamic power.[54]

This was a clear declaration of Cram's core belief. His message was not encouraging, perhaps, but he still held out hope of redemption through religion. The issue grew in relevance to him as he considered the decline of religion in society.

In response to growing attacks from the proponents of industrialized architecture and criticism of his work as eclectic and old fashioned, Cram felt obliged to defend his legacy. "Does this conspectus of architectural history indicate uncertainty and lack of conviction on the part of its authors?" he asked rhetorically. "Does it imply opportunism without seriousness of purpose and void of principle? I think otherwise."[55] He went on to defend his use of Gothic, claiming it was not a style at all but a spirit. "Organic" and "vital," the Gothic encompassed infinite design possibilities. "I cannot help reiterating that Gothic (and every other valid architectural style, for that matter) is just as much a matter of structural integrity as it is of artistic design," Cram wrote. He continued,

In the case of Gothic this organic synthesis is even more intimate and unavoidable than elsewhere, for it is the most delicately articulated, the most physically complicated of any style, with its concentrated loads, its balanced thrusts and its, so to speak, arboreal development from roots to trunk, branches, twigs, leaves and flowers. . . . The measure of a Gothic church is absolutely organic; it associates itself with, takes hold on, the universal laws of life itself.[56]

As the most prominent firm in Boston from 1920 to 1940, the Cram office saw many young architects pass through from Harvard and MIT to careers in other American cities; through them Cram's Gothic principles quickened American architecture of all stylistic bents. Raymond Hood in Philadelphia, Samuel E. Lunden in Los Angeles, William Ward Watkin in Houston, and many others went on from Cram & Ferguson to teach and practice in their respective cities (fig. I-41).

By the end of the 1920s, Cram and Bess had moved to their Sudbury home, Whitehall. Cram had purchased the 200-acre estate with its colonial farmhouse in 1906, and added, over the years, to the stately home where George Washington had once slept. Cram wrote that the sense of land ownership was "something that had no rival, except the allied desire for children."[57] He spent happy hours working in the gardens, an enthusiasm akin to his taste for medieval Christian pleasures. He quoted Sir Francis Bacon: "God Almighty first planted a garden and indeed it is the purest of human pleasures. It is the greatest refreshment to the spirit of man."[58]

Over the years, Cram added to the property a porch befitting an antebellum southern plantation and a large library that held some four thousand books, among them a complete collection of the works of John Ruskin from his father's library, Dugdale's *Monasticon*, Taine's *Histories*, Gasquet, Belloc, and St. Augustine. The elaborate Gothic world that he had created largely in his imagination had been made possible by books, and he was never more at home than when he was surrounded by them.

The Crams' social circle continued to shrink, but Cram worked virtually to the end of his life, except when he and Bess were traveling. They went to warm places in winter—the Bahamas, Arizona, South Carolina. He was removed from his once-active part in the city scene (he never learned to drive).

John Doran, whose memories of Cram were the last, recalled, "I had little contact with him outside the office. Always he was deeply engrossed in his work and seemingly interested in nothing else. It may well have been that he was quite different in his smaller office of earlier times. Certainly there is ample testimony that outside the office especially with his peers he was a talkative and amusing companion."[59]

Doran remembered Cram's formality. He addressed everyone in the office as "Mister," and naturally expected the same respect for himself. Dressed in his blue smock, Cram stopped at every drafting table to watch the work in progress. As he inspected this work, he was usually silent, hardly ever critical, although he might later turn to a partner and remark, "Colonial is a completely artificial style".[60]

Never losing his commitment to the Gothic, he believed that the colonial consisted of a set repertoire of classical references to be assembled, relatively at random. But he also understood that colonial architecture was popular and made the office very prosperous indeed.

The firm recorded new projects after the stock market crash of October 1929 —a large project for Boston University and church work, including the Mellon family's East Liberty Presbyterian in Pittsburgh—but most were abandoned or left uncompleted in the following Depression years. The firm, like many others, undertook Works Progress Administration commissions, serving as architectural consultant for the bridges over Cape Cod Canal at Bourne and Sandwich, both of which received a 1936 design award from the American Institute of Steel Construction.

Cram continued to insist that architectural currents were closely associated with social trends, putting him in a position, some thought, to make sweeping historical observations. This he did in the *American Mercury*, edited by H. L. Mencken. In a 1932 essay for the maga-

I-41. Cram shares a bottle of wine with Raymond Hood in Bermuda, about 1930. (HDB/Cram & Ferguson Archive)

I-42. Cram critiques work on the Doheny Library at USC, Los Angeles, California, 1932, with Sam Lunden (to Cram's right) as staff take notes. (HDB/Cram & Ferguson Archive; photo: Adelbert Bartlett)

zine, Cram's wrote: "And why do we not behave like human beings? For by and large we certainly do not. Regard dispassionately the history of what we call 'civilization.' . . . It is a farrago of cruelty, slaughter and injustice."[61] His premise that society had not improved measurably since Nero and Genghis Khan led him to the conclusion that Darwin's notion of progressive evolution was flawed. Society did not improve as time marched forth. Gas warfare and the "advancing technological and capitalist civilization" were proof of that—proof, too, that the medieval heyday should not be discounted merely because it was four centuries in the past.[62]

Cram's last Gothic work, executed with Chester Brown, was the monastery chapel for the Society of St. John the Evangelist, the Cowley Fathers, in Cambridge, completed in 1938. The chapel reflects the refined simplicity of a mature architect. Its most awe-inspiring touch may be the cool blue light from clerestory windows that falls gently on the rough granite of the walls and the polished marble of the pavement. It received the 1939 Harleston Parker

Award from the Boston Society of Architects as the most beautiful building of the year.

At the same time, the firm accepted and completed a commercial building with unmistakable modern influences—not too different, perhaps, from those that Cram might have deplored in the past—and he deplored this one. The design for the New England Life Insurance Company headquarters in Boston was a stripped-down classical building, its tower garnished with Grecian funerary urns. If Cram himself did not intend this ornament as lighthearted or even ironic, others interpreted it as such, including the wit that wrote the clerihew:

> Ralph Adams Cram
> One morning said damn
> And designed an urn burial
> For a concern actuarial.[63]

Modern culture was a travesty to Cram. And soon World War II—modernism's inevitable result as far as he was concerned—brought renewed hard times for architecture, and for Cram & Ferguson. Work came to a virtual standstill at the office, except for projects for the defense department. Cram was alone and depressed when he wrote to his granddaughter Pat on December 18, 1941, that he had "no memory left, I go to the office and only four men are left, the rest have been drafted."[64]

Nine months later, on September 22, 1942, Ralph Adams Cram died. Obituaries appeared in major national newspapers, and even President Roosevelt noted his passing. Despite Cram's prominence, the Rockingham (New Hampshire) *Times*, lamenting his loss, predicted the full eclipse of his reputation: "Among the greater men of our nation, men who by their capacity in their chosen calling have contributed great things, Cram is the One Major Forgotten Man, his biography has never been written."[65]

Years later, John Doran described Cram's funeral, which took place on a beautiful autumn day,

I thought how significant it was that he should have chosen to be buried from the old parish church where he had been baptized (by his old friend Bishop Brent), which is not a very grand affair. He is buried in Sudbury by his small fieldstone chapel. I have thought since, on hearing of architects given splendid ceremonies in their great churches, and being buried in a crypt of their vast cathedrals, that is was typical of Mr. Cram to have wanted none of this."[66]

Doran noted that many associates and former associates were there, many of whom had lost touch with their former mentor. "One did not, I suppose, have to know Ralph Adams Cram very well to realize his worth or significance. He had brought into all our lives, however remotely, something quite remarkable which we would never forget."[67]

The service was an opportunity for those who had worked with Cram to think deeply about a life that influenced each one of them. Many of them, most in fact, had moved beyond the belief that Gothic was the only style worth considering. But none could ignore the larger ideas that obsessed Cram throughout his whole career, and his quest to tie elements of the past with his fond, if quixotic, hopes for the future. Despite his sense that he lived to see his most revered values degraded, Cram achieved a prodigious success. From modest beginnings as the son of a minister, he lived his life in a whirl of European travel, among his books, and always at work on projects that were interesting and challenging. His writings might leave the impression that he was indeed an eccentric character, but the truth was otherwise.

Today, many of the values that Cram held dear—human scale, handcrafted detail, and respect for tradition and the lessons of history—guide architects and their clients, and the best of his work is again treasured for its originality and timelessness. The firm he founded continues in Boston today, restoring and adding to his buildings and occasionally working in his beloved Gothic style.

NOTES

1. Ralph Adams Cram. *Gothic Quest*. (New York: Baker, Taylor & Co. 1907), 10.
2. Ralph Adams Cram. *My Life in Architecture*. (Boston: Little, Brown and Company, 1936), 28.
3. Ralph Adams Cram. *Church Building*. 3rd ed. (Boston: Small, Maynard & Co., 1914), 45.
4. *Rockingham News*. Undated fragment Courtesy of Hampton Historical Society.
5. John Ruskin. *Mornings in Florence*. (London: George Allen, 1904), 96.
6. Cram, *My Life in Architecture*, 53.
7. Ibid, 57.
8. Ibid, 61.
9. Ibid, 66.
10. Ibid, 168.
11. Ibid, 70.
12. Ibid, 76.
13. Ibid, 77.
14. Ibid, 78.
15. Charles Wentworth, *Letter to Ralph Adams Cram*, undated.
16. Cram, *My Life in Architecture*, 72.
17. Henry-Russell Hitchcock, *Architecture: Ninteenth and Twentieth Centuries*. The Pelican History of Art. Ed. Nikolaus Pevsner. (New York: Penguin Books, 1978), 542.
18. Cram, *My Life in Architecture*, 74.
19. Douglas Shand-Tucci. *Built in Boston: City and Suburb 1800-1950*.(New York: New York Graphic Society, 1978) 159.
20. Cram, *My Life in Architecture*, 84.
21. Ibid, 90.
22. Ibid.
23. Ralph Adams Cram. *Church Building*. 3rd ed. (Boston: Small, Maynard & Company, 1914), 2.
24. Ibid.
25. Cram. *My Life in Architecture*, 100.
26. Ibid, 102.
27. Ibid, 106.
28. Ibid.
29. Ibid, 105.
30. Ibid.
31. Montgomery Schuyler, "The Work of Cram, Goodhue & Ferguson," *The Architectural Record*, XXIX (January, 1911), 87, quoted in Robert Muccigrosso, *American Gothic: The Mind and Art of Ralph Adams Cram* (Washington, D.C.: University Press of America, 1980), 82.
32. Charles Moore. *Daniel H. Burnham: Architect Planner of Cities, I* (Boston: Houghton Mifflin Co., 1921), 196, quoted in Robert Muccigrosso, *American Gothic: The Mind and Art of Ralph Adams Cram* (Washington, D.C.: University Press of America, 1980), 81.
33. Cram. *My Life in Architecture*, 108.
34. Ralph Adams Cram. *The Ruined Abbeys of Great Britain*. (New York: James Pott & Company, 1905), 1.
35. Cram, *My Life in Architecture*, 187.
36. Ralph Adams Cram. *Letter to his mother*, S. B. Cram, 1904.
37. Ralph Adams Cram. *Letter to his wife, Bess Cram*, 1907.
38. Goodhue. Letter to a student, c.1912
39. Henry-Russell Hitchcock. *Architecture: Ninteenth and Twentieth Centuries*. The Pelican History of Art. Ed. Nikolaus Pevsner.(New York: Penguin Books, 1978), 546.
40. Ibid.
41. Annie Ray Watkin, interview by author at her summer home, Kennebunkport, Maine, 2000.
42. Richard Oliver, *Bertram Grosvenor Goodhue*. American Monograph Series. Edited by Robert A. M. Stern (New York: The Architectural History Foundation, 1983; Cambridge, Massachusetts and London: The MIT Press, 1983), 120–121.
43. Cram. "Bertram Grosvenor Goodhue— Architect and Master of Many Arts." *AIA Press*, 1925, 32.
44. Robert Muccigrosso, *American Gothic: The Mind and Art of Ralph Adams Cram* (Washington, D.C.: University Press of America, 1980), 153.
45. Cram, *The Gothic Quest*, 342–343, quoted in Muccigrosso, *American Gothic: The Mind and Art of Ralph Adams Cram*, 152.
46. Cram, *My Life in Architecture*, 209.
47. Ibid, 205.
48. Ralph Adams Cram. *Walled Towns*. (Boston: Marshall, Jones & Company, 1919), 29.
49. Ralph Adams Cram. *The Substance of Gothic: Six Lectures on the Development of Architecture from Charlemagne to Henry VIII*. 2nd ed. (Boston: Marshall Jones Company, 1925), 3.
50. Ralph Adams Cram. *The Nemesis of Mediocrity*. (Boston: Marshall Jones Company, 1917), 27.
51. Ralph Adams Cram, "The Test of Beauty," *Harvard Graduate's Magazine*, September 1921 vol. XXX, no. CXVII, 2.
52. Ralph Adams Cram, "The Spanish Notes" *American Architect*, January 1924, vol. CXXV, No. 2437, 47.
53. Cram. *Church Building*, 276.
54. Cram, Ralph Adams. "Some Architectural and Spiritual Aspects of the Chapel: The Challenge Offered by Princeton's New Edifice, and the Answer Which the Future Can Give It." *The Princeton Alumni Weekly*, May 25, 1928, 987.
55. Cram. *My Life in Architecture*, 238.
56. Ibid, 182.
57. Ibid, 229.
58. Ibid, 232.
59. John Doran. Undated letter, HDB archive.
60. Ibid.
61. American Mercury Manuscript, 1932.
62. Ibid.
63. Walter Muir Whitehall. *Boston: A Topographical History*. 2nd ed. (Cambridge, Massachusetts: The Belknapp Press of Harvard University Press, 1968), 189.
64. Ralph Adams Cram, Letter to Mary Cram, 1941.
65. *Rockingham News*. 1942 Fragment Courtesy of Hampton Historical Society.
66. John Doran. Undated letter, HDB archive.
67. Ibid.

2. Religious Architecture

From that fateful moment in Rome on Christmas Eve when Cram had his epiphany, he knew that he would design buildings meant for spiritual purposes. And in doing that he believed he was bringing to people a higher experience, one of beauty and awe.

Cram's churches range from the simple chapel he built for himself in a field behind his country house at Whitehall to the grandest, most awe-inspiring structures ever built in the United States for the purpose of worship, like East Liberty Presbyterian Church in Pittsburgh and the Cathedral of St John the Divine in New York City. The spaces, both the largest and the most humble, are infused with a quiet, spiritual atmosphere. Visitors are welcome, without regard to the religious tradition they bring, and Cram's wish that the disparate churches could be fused into one unified church is at least realized in this one experience—differences are erased in the common sense of awe and wonder elicited by the buildings.

The exteriors of Cram's churches are varied: some are less than fully inspiring and this is pur-poseful because Cram, like the medieval builders he admired, cared first for the experience of the interior and was sometimes willing to sacrifice a lithe exterior for the simplicity and power of the interior. This accorded with a real functionalism in Cram's outlook, that the form of an object should be most distinguished by its fitness for its purpose.

The churches shown in this section include commissions for which Cram was responsible for all or most of a new or renovated building. The firm records are incomplete and all but one of the firm's job books are lost, making it difficult to identify the full extent of Cram's oeuvre. New interest in Cram has resulted in many requests to verify his authorship of buildings across the United States, sometimes leading to the rediscovery of churches not explicitly mentioned in the firm's records or for which the name has changed (for example, St. Andrew's in Denver, Colorado, previously named Trinity.)

Religious buildings on academic campuses are included in the academic section.

All Saints Church Ashmont
Dorchester, Massachusetts, 1891

Colonel and Mrs. Oliver Peabody were en route to services at their church, King's Chapel in Boston, when a blizzard caused them to pull their carriage up to the wood-frame roadside chapel that then housed the All Saints parish in Ashmont. The sermon was about the loss of children and the Peabodys, whose only daughter had recently died, were deeply moved. They joined the parish and later donated the money for a new church. The great success of the design and its subsequent promotion by the firm helped to establish the firm as an emerging power in ecclesiastical design.

In an 1899 article in *The Churchman*, Cram explained that he had rejected the Classical and Romanesque because those styles expressed conditions utterly unlike those that now prevailed.

The times demanded the romance and mystery of the Gothic.

All Saints exterior suggests a debt to a variety of English precedents, including the towers of Bodley's and St. Swithun's Quadrangle at Magdalen College, Oxford; the low-sloped roof suggests St. George's, Windsor. The mass of the tower is the culmination of a formal hierarchy that begins with the diminutive Saxon porch. In the interior design of All Saints, the firm began to use the forms it would refine in the years to come. Most notable is the vertical emphasis, raising the altar to an unusual height, space rising into the tower at the west end of the nave where a large window lit into the rear of the nave. The modern introduction of a large organ loft in the tower space diminished the effect. (see also Fig. I-16.)

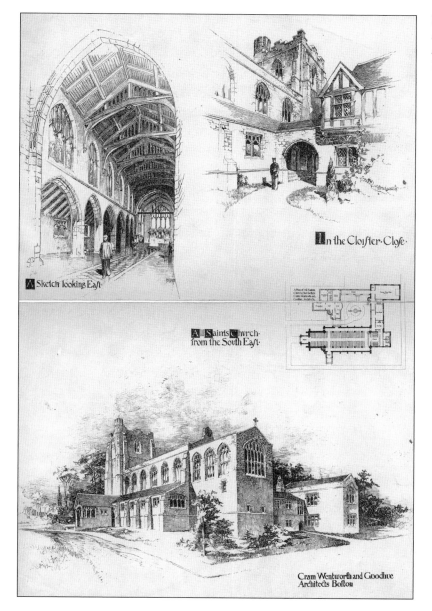

Rendering. (HDB/Cram & Ferguson Archive, office reprint from *American Architect & Building News*, August 13, 1892)

St. Paul's Episcopal Church
Brockton, Massachusetts, 1891–94

Shortly after the completion of All Saints Ashmont, Cram, Wentworth and Goodhue received commissions for three additional Gothic churches in the Boston area: St Paul's Brockton, the Swedenborgian Church in Newton, and St. Stephen's in Cohasset. Cram's developing vision of a formal liturgy, first attempted in the design of All Saints Ashmont and developed in these three churches, became the foundation of much of the firm's design work that followed. Formal procession demanded long naves enclosed between bearing stone walls; stone arcades supported rich, dark timber roofs and created processional aisles for the return file from receiving the Eucharist, unusual in the Protestant church of the day. The chancel, separated from the nave by a proscenium arch or rude beam, was clad with richly carved oak paneling and outfitted with a high altar and a reredos. The plan usually included a bell tower, in the village churches to a side or on a corner. These were sometimes left unfinished because funds were lacking—as was the case, for example, at St. Andrew's (Denver) and St. Paul's Malden and Brockton.

Rendering. (HDB/Cram & Ferguson Archive, office reprint from *American Architect & Building News*, Oct. 3, 1892)

Swedenborgian Church
Newton, Massachusetts, c. 1893

Newton Swedenborgian repeats the proto-turret from All Saints Ashmont with the tower now off to the side and out of proportion to the wide nave adjacent. The tower entry first attempted in this church was perfected in the Second Congregatioal Church in Exeter, New Hampshire (see page 48).

The tower and its entry. (HDB/Cram & Ferguson Archive; photo: Sarah Bradford)

Church of Saints Peter and Paul
Fall River, Massachusetts, c. 1893

Cram experimented with Italian Renaissance themes here for his first Catholic church. The high engaged altar and elaborate baldachin are overpowered by the fruited baroque decoration around the pediment, an uncommon theme in Cram churches. Saints Peter and Paul burned in 1973.

Interior. (HDB/Cram & Ferguson Archive;
photo: Arthur C. Haskell)

Christ Church
Hyde Park, Massachusetts, 1893

One of the first in the series of Gothic churches the office designed, Christ Church shows the influence of St. Mary's Church, Iffley, Oxfordshire, in the massive buttresses that frame an uncomfortable, tentative entrance porch.

Facade. (HDB/Cram & Ferguson Archive; photo: Ethan Anthony)

Nave, view toward the chancel screen. (HDB/Cram & Ferguson Archive; photo: Ethan Anthony)

St. Luke's Church
Roxbury, Massachusetts, 1895

This little-known early church was consecrated by Bishop Lawrence. Probably a church of Cram's life-long friend Charles Henry Brent (1862–1929), whose tombstone Cram also designed. Brent, like Cram, was a *Time* Magazine cover in August 1927 and a close friend of General Pershing. Brent may have been the connection for Cram to President Howard Taft. Brent was with Taft on his arrival in the Philippines in 1902, following the Spanish-American War. Shortly thereafter, Taft appointed Cram, Goodhue and Ferguson as architects of the Washington Hotel in Colón, Panama. The firm also served as architects to President Taft's brother's Taft School in 1912.

Entry facade. (HDB/Cram & Ferguson Archive; photo: Ethan Anthony)

Second Congregational Church
(Phillips Church)
Exeter, New Hampshire, 1895–98

The cornerstone for the Second Congregational Church was laid October 13, 1897. The church was built to serve the Second Congregational Church on land donated by Phillips Exeter Academy, and around the base of the building are inscribed the names of colleges and universities that were conceivably the primary objective of the Academy graduates.

The rugged buttresses and pointed arched windows of the exterior belie the expansive simplicity of the interior. A spired tower was to be at the midpoint on one side of the nave but the full plan was never built, leaving the tower occupying a corner between the nave and the fellowship hall wing. This resulted in a more powerful composition than the full plan might have offered: the major plan elements rotate around the tower entry and stair. The two-story volume connects the nave to the two floors of the fellowship wing.

Beneath the "Catholic" exterior, uncharacteristic of a New England religious institution at the time, is a Protestant lecture hall measuring forty by ninety feet. It consisted of one space without side aisles, the unusually broad span achieved with wrought-iron tension rods supporting the roof carefully concealed in faux wooden trusses.

View of church. (HDB/Cram & Ferguson Archive; photo: Greg Premru, 2003)

St. Stephen's Episcopal Church
Cohasset, Massachusetts, 1899

Sited on a powerful outcropping, St. Stephen's dominates views from the center of Cohasset. The model for St. Stephen's was St. Mary the Virgin, Eaton Bray, Dunstable, England, a church Cram had photographed for his *English Country Churches*.

The bell tower of St. Stephen's appears to grow up organically from the ledge of its site. The tower is longer on the north/south than on the east/west axis. Its slender profile, viewed against the long elevation of the nave, accentuates the power of the entire composition, an early example of the sub-

tlety of Cram's massing and composition.

A comparison of the west elevations of three early churches demonstrates Cram's experimentation with figure and ground in their composition: at All Saints the window and surrounding wall occupy equal widths of wall. At Exeter the window is narrower relative to the wall but the introduction of a western door and buttresses creates the most powerful elevation of the three. At St. Stephen's the west window has become almost inconsequential in the elevation.

View of church from road (left) and south side and porch. (HDB/Cram & Ferguson Archive)

West door of St. Stephen's, overlooking the village below. This area is now overgrown, so the door opens onto a thicket and is unused. (HDB/Cram & Ferguson Archive)

East elevation, 1992. The entry door is on the south side, through a traditional lychgate. That this was Cram's intent is clear from the plan. (Photo: Ethan Anthony)

Plan. (HDB/Cram & Ferguson Archive)

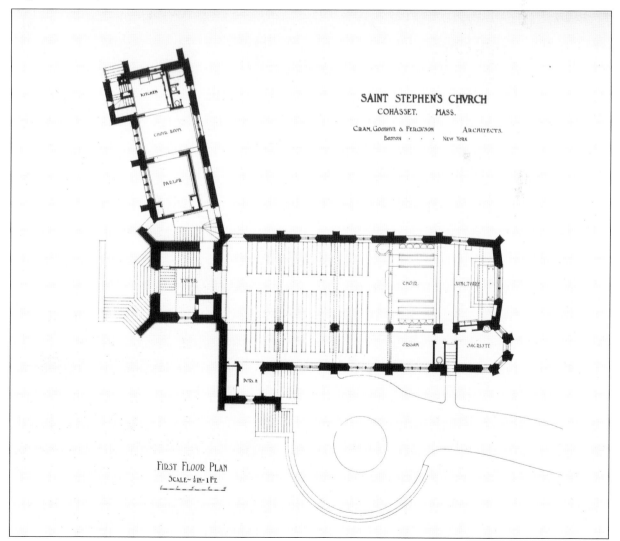

Emmanuel Church
Newport, Rhode Island, 1900

The first of several projects Cram and Goodhue designed for the John Nicholas Brown family, Emmanuel Church was not awarded lightly. Cram and Goodhue submitted a sketch in competition with several other firms. Cram's accompanying letter, dated September 10, 1900, states, "I quite understand your disinclination to decide on us or any other firm of architects in the dark, and your desire to see sketches from several firms before reaching a decision is perfectly reasonable particularly in view of the fact that you express your willingness to pay whatever small sum might be necessary for obtaining sketches. . . ."

The almost flat roof and offset bell tower are features not found on many other Cram churches. The tower placement echoes that of Queens Chapel at Magdalen College, Oxford. This is one of the few early churches in which Cram and Goodhue attempted this arrangement, probably because the massing possibilities were so limited in a smaller group of buildings with the tower in this location. Also unusual is the combination of a prominent colonnade and vestigial aisle that contributes to the very vertical feel of the nave. (HDB/Cram & Ferguson Archive; photo: Paul J. Weber)

Nave, looking east. As at All Saints Ashmont (see page 42), the chancel floor is elevated and dominated by a powerful vertical window and reredos. The chancel is wrapped in rich linen-fold paneling; painted saints and angels cover the plaster portions of wall above. (HDB/Cram & Ferguson Archive; photo: Paul J. Weber)

Nave, looking to the west lancet windows. (HDB/Cram & Ferguson Archive; photo: Paul J. Weber)

St. Paul's Episcopal Church
Chicago, Illinois, 1902

The foundation of St. Paul's had been built to the design of a local architect when the new rector of St. Paul's decided to change architects. Cram, Goodhue and Ferguson's design fit the existing foundation, but the height of the nave was reduced to save money. Cram ignored the resulting building. No plans, photos or record of the project survive in the office; fire destroyed the church in 1956.

Exterior. This is the only surviving image of St. Paul's, reproduced from a church record that was lost in the conflagration. (Courtesy of the parisioners of St. Paul's)

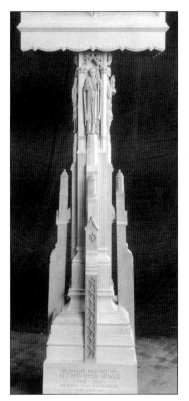

Lectern designed for St. Paul's. (HDB/Cram & Ferguson Archive)

First Baptist Church
Pittsburgh, Pennsylvania, 1902

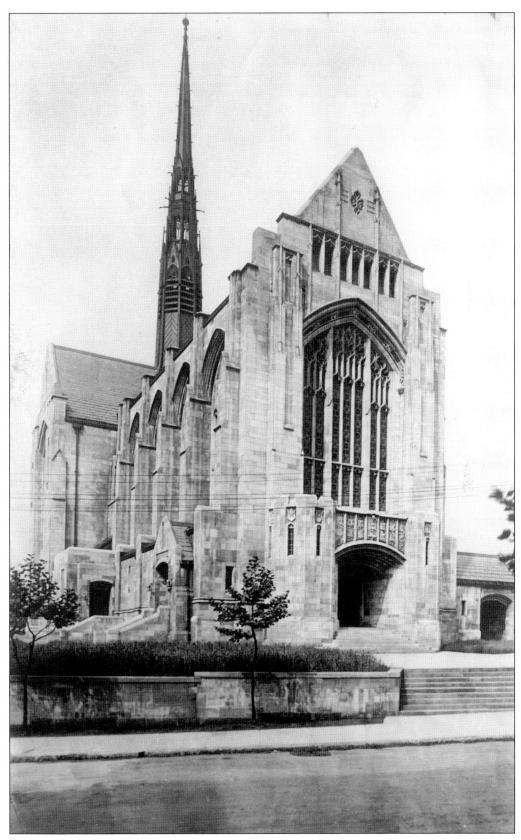

First Baptist, designed by Goodhue, shows Cram's influence in the stark gable and galleried front. It is the first appearance of a copper-clad fleche. Goodhue's hand can be seen in the modeled west porch. (HDB/Cram & Ferguson Archive)

All Saints Chapel, University of the South
Sewanee, Tennessee, 1903

The design for Sewanee was not realized until nearly thirty years after it was commissioned, and then with many of the details altered, not for the better. But the scale of the original survived, as did the interior as Cram envisioned it. The exterior has many fussy archaeologically derived details inorganically applied.

As at Emmanuel Church, the tower at Sewanee is separate from the nave, but here the arrangement is more clearly based on Queens Chapel, Oxford, and the tower may be seen as an early attempt at a very large freestanding tower with a church that is on a cathedral scale. The placement of the tower, while less powerful, avoided placing the enormous mass on the crossing piers and the foundation that would be required to support this force.

Original design of the chapel. (HDB/Cram & Ferguson Archive)

Christ Church Cathedral Competition
Victoria, British Columbia, 1903 (project)

Cram and Goodhue entered many competitions they did not win. The large number of cathedral competitions in the first years of their practice gave the young design team many opportunities to perfect new ideas they used in later commissions. The design for Christ Church Cathedral was based on Cram's study of the Tintern Abbey ruins, which also provided the basis for the 1905 design of Calvary Pittsburgh and the later St. Paul's Malden (see pages 64 and 86).

Rendering by Cram. (From Ralph Adams Cram, *Church Building*, 3rd ed. Boston: Maynard & Co., 1914)

St. John in the Wilderness Episcopal Cathedral
Denver, Colorado, 1903 (project)

Cram, Goodhue and Ferguson were invited to enter the competition for the Denver cathedral along with two other firms, evidence of the distance their fame had spread. (Tracy and Swartwout of New York City won the commission.) The competition scheme was similar to that for the Cadet Chapel at West Point and the later design of All Saints Cathedral in Nova Scotia (see page 62).

The firm was designing churches large enough to support a great tower over the crossing and this appealed to Cram, who wished to revive the forms from the great abbey churches such as Glastonbury and Whitby Abbey, which, like St. John, both had a great tower over the crossing.

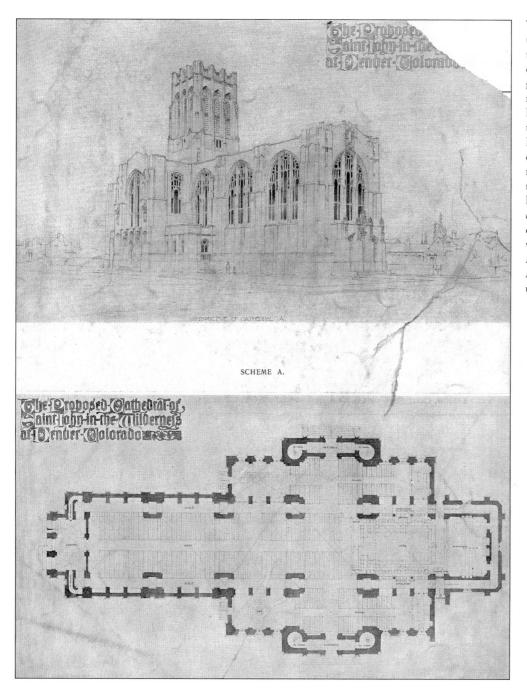

SCHEME A.

The firm's entry. The massive volumetric quality of the nave contrasts with the soaring vertical elements of the tower and the great window. Windows of the nave were to be high above eye level, giving the whole composition the effect of rising upward. Doubled buttresses at the tower corners presage Goodhue's use of rounded towers to emphasize the mass of the central towers and fin-like free-standing buttresses subdivide the west entry doors, extending up into the great west window. (HDB/Cram & Ferguson Archive), office reprint from *American Architect and Builder*, undated)

First Unitarian Church
West Newton, Massachusetts, 1905

Here Cram adapted the English monastery plan to the neighborhood church. The passage from parish house to church is oblique, with shifts in direction and elevation as one moves through a succession of spaces.

The Saxon, half-timber Parish House connects to the church forming a cloister garth. Access to the courtyard is through an arched opening at the base of the bell tower. (HDB/Cram & Ferguson Archive; photo: R. M. Shaw)

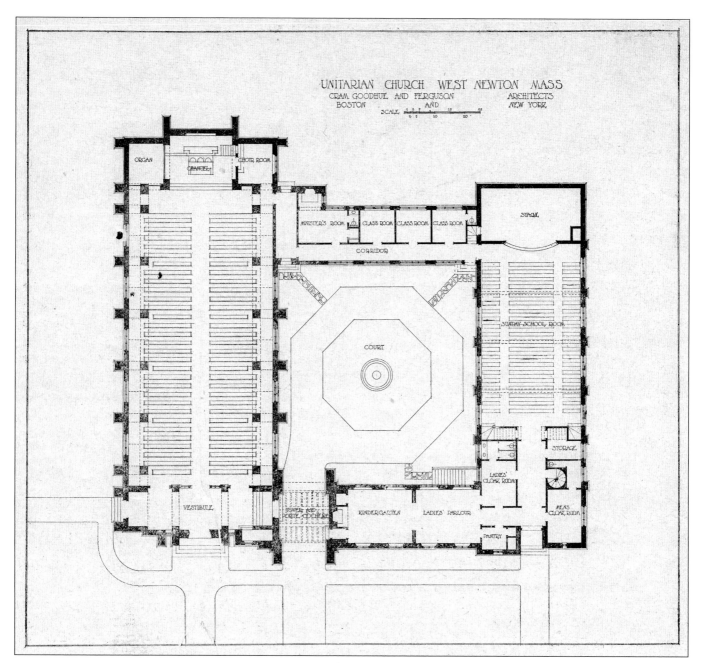

UNITARIAN CHURCH WEST NEWTON MASS
CRAM GOODHUE AND FERGUSON ARCHITECTS
BOSTON AND NEW YORK
SCALE

ORGAN
CHANCEL
CHOIR ROOM

MINISTER'S ROOM
CLASS ROOM
CLASS ROOM
CLASS ROOM

STAGE

CORRIDOR

SUNDAY SCHOOL ROOM

COURT

STORAGE

VESTIBULE

TOWER AND
PORTE COCHERE

KINDERGARTEN

LADIES' PARLOUR

LADIES'
CLOAK ROOM

MEN'S
CLOAK ROOM

PANTRY

Plan of Unitarian Church.
(HDB/Cram & Ferguson Archive)

Westminster Presbyterian Church
Springfield, Illinois, 1905

Cram's first Presbyterian church is Gothic, despite his protestations that it was an inappropriate style for a Protestant church. Westminster Presbyterian and Calvary Pittsburgh both borrowed the triple lancet west windows from Whitby Abbey, a ruin that provided material for many Cram designs.

Exterior. (HDB/Cram & Ferguson Archive;
photo: Herbert Georg Studios)

All Saints Cathedral
Halifax, Nova Scotia, 1906

Efforts to build a stately new cathedral for Halifax began during the reign of Queen Victoria, when the bishop commissioned the distinguished British architect A. S. Street, mentor of Richard Norman Shaw, to design a Gothic cathedral. Local resistance to the modernism of the Street design resulted in a second competition won by Cram, Goodhue and Ferguson. Goodhue was the author of the firm's entry and also of the accompanying letter explaining that the design attempted to "produce a building, which though not large, should contain the requisites, both in plan and in effect, of a Cathedral rather than a church." The judge, a professor from McGill University, selected the Goodhue design entry, apparently for its tower, which he said was worthy of a cathedral. He also said that the "relation of the main fabric to subsidiary buildings contemplated for the future is finely realized." His main objection to the design was that it appeared to cost more than the $150,000 that the diocese had allocated; the diocese indeed could not afford the design. Construction of the tower was postponed and never completed.

Goodhue sketches made during his visit to see the site. (Courtesy of All Saints Cathedral Archives)

Rendering of final design by Bertram Goodhue.
As built, the cathedral was two bays shorter. (HDB/
Cram & Ferguson Archive, from *The Architects &
Their Works*, vol. I, no. II, Oct. 24, 1908)

Photo of church in 2001. (Courtesy of All Saints
Cathedral Archives; photo: William Naftel)

Calvary Episcopal Church
Pittsburgh, Pennsylvania, 1906

Cram and Goodhue each submitted a design for Calvary Episcopal that demonstrate the difference between them at this point; Cram's won. (Goodhue's is shown on page 28.) Cram's demonstrates his mastery of proportion in a smooth and volumetric expression. It foreshadows a more modern approach by the firm, even though the antecedent was a simple Cistercian abbey that Cram sketched for his book *The Ruined Abbeys of Great Britain*. Of this church Cram wrote in an undated letter to his mother that it was the "best we have ever done, or shall do."

Exterior View.
(From *Church Building*, 3rd ed.)

Chancel view of Calvary Episcopal Church showing one of Cram's first carved Rood screens. (HDB/Cram & Ferguson Archive; Photo: Joanne Devereaux)

Calvary features a large clerestory with triplet stained glass windows by Cram collaborator Charles Connick. (HDB/Cram & Ferguson Archive; Photo: Joanne Devereaux)

Glens Falls Presbyterian Church
Glens Falls, New York, 1906

The Glens Falls church, in a "Presbyterian style," is similar to a group of Massachusetts churches by the firm located in Hyde Park, Malden, and Brockton. The west front is modeled on contemporary work by Sedding and Prior, specifically Sedding's Holy Trinity in Chelsea, London. Flanking porches house twin stairs leading to a balcony above the entry and screening the aisles beyond. Similar porches of varying sizes and shapes are a feature of the west front design of most of the firm's later Presbyterian churches.

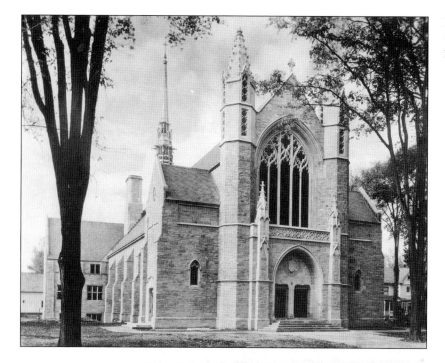

Exterior showing flanking porches. (HDB/Cram & Ferguson Archive; photo: Paul J. Weber)

Many Cram floor plans placed seating in aisles with substantial pillars supporting the arcade, blocking the view of the altar. Cram evidently did not feel this was a problem. (HDB/Cram & Ferguson Archive; photo: Paul J. Weber)

St. Thomas Episcopal Church
New York, New York, 1907

The St. Thomas commission came to the firm in 1907, two years after a fire destroyed the church of this important Episcopal parish in Manhattan. Although Cram, Goodhue and Ferguson were the unanimous choice of the selection committee, a fierce competition over design soon arose within the firm. Simmering administrative disagreements between Cram and Goodhue had evolved into artistic disputes. Midway through the design process, and after a bitter exchange, the partners agreed to submit two schemes to the committee, which ultimately chose Cram's. This was the first blow in the seven-year quarrel that finally led to the dissolution of the partnership.

Cram's version as built. The facade is divided between a massive tower on the corner of Fifth Avenue at 53rd Street and the entrance to the nave. Sedding's influence can be seen in the expression of the buttresses as tracery. (HDB/Cram & Ferguson Archive)

Two schemes for the east end of St. Thomas, in renderings by E. Donald Robb—Cram's on the left; Goodhue's on the right. Aspects of each were adopted in the final design. Cram's design featured a long, open gallery along the left side of the nave, an asymmetry that Goodhue condemned, in a letter to his partner, as "an extremely objectionable feature." In fact, the asymmetry of the interior echoes that of the facade. The competition committee regarded the gallery as useful overflow seating for the large urban parish. (HDB/Cram & Ferguson Archive; photos: Richard Creek)

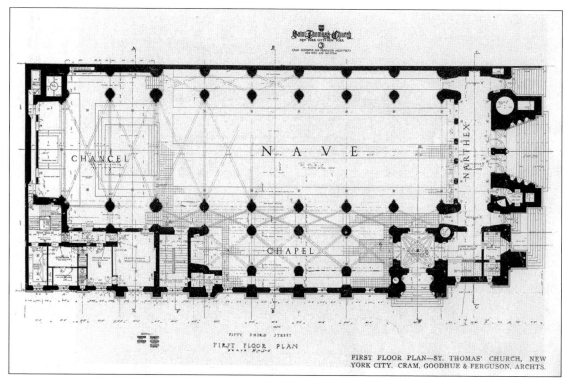

Plan. (HDB/Cram & Ferguson Archive, office reprint from *Architectural Record*, date unknown)

Nave. (HDB/Cram & Ferguson Archive;
photo: John Wallace Gillies)

Trinity Memorial Church (now St. Andrew's)
Denver, Colorado, 1907

Although the firm's submission for the Denver cathedral was not successful, the competition led to a commission for a small urban parish church, Trinity Memorial. Augustus DuPont donated the initial funding in memory of the first Bishop of Colorado, whose home church had been Trinity in Boston. The office designed two churches featuring a blocky western tower bluntly terminated by a spire or fleche. First Presbyterian in Oakland, California (see page 96), was completed but at Trinity funds ran out and construction had to be halted with the tower incomplete.

Trinity is an eclectic mix of elements: the clerestory windows are early decorated Gothic, the nave windows Norman lancets; the west window is geometrical and the porch window is curvilinear.

View in 2000 of the Cram church (right) and the later parish house by Denver architect Jacques Benedict. (Photo: Ethan Anthony)

Church of the Covenant
Cleveland, Ohio, 1907

Cram exaggerated the twin towers, buttresses, and other elements that he used with greater sensitivity in previous work, such as First Presbyterian and Glens Falls (see page 66). Goodhue's absence in New York may explain such an unsuccessful experiment with relative proportions.

Front elevation. (HDB/Cram & Ferguson Archive; photo: William H. Pierce)

St. Paul's Episcopal Cathedral
Detroit, Michigan, 1908–11

St. Paul's was designed in the Boston office when Cram's relationship with Goodhue had begun to deteriorate; it shows Cram's heavier and more explosive hand. The tower was never completed, however, St Paul's is one of the few Cram designs to have realized flying buttresses. With Goodhue's influence missing, the proportions and massing demonstrate a new power and dynamism.

St. Paul's as built, with its incomplete central tower. (HDB/Cram & Ferguson Archive)

Transept. (HDB/Cram & Ferguson Archive; photo: Wm. Kvenzel)

High altar and east window. (HDB/Cram & Ferguson Archive; photo: Paul J. Weber)

West end of nave with rose window. (HDB/Cram & Ferguson Archive)

Church and Rectory
Guantanamo, Cuba, 1908 (project)

This is one of a group of churches the firm designed based on Mexican architecture and elements of Spanish Plateresque and Churriguerresque styles, which Goodhue observed during his trips to Mexico. Along with the later Washington Hotel (see page 218), this dramatic departure from the firm's English Arts and Crafts roots accorded perfectly with the movement's ideal of seeking vernacular models.

The most distinctive characteristic of the Cuban churches is their overall plainness contrasting with a few elaborately ornamented features, such as the main door frame and bell tower vents.

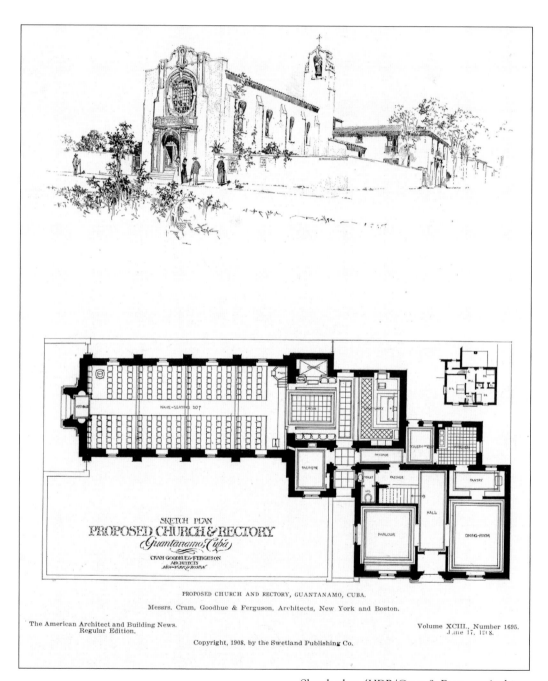

SKETCH PLAN
PROPOSED CHURCH & RECTORY
Guantanamo, Cuba
CRAM GOODHUE & FERGUSON
ARCHITECTS
NEW YORK & BOSTON

PROPOSED CHURCH AND RECTORY, GUANTANAMO, CUBA.

Messrs. Cram, Goodhue & Ferguson, Architects, New York and Boston.

The American Architect and Building News.
Regular Edition.

Volume XCIII., Number 1695.
June 17, 1908.

Copyright, 1908, by the Swetland Publishing Co.

Sketch plan. (HDB/Cram & Ferguson Archive, office reprint from *American Architect & Building News*, June 17, 1908)

Russell Sage Memorial First Presbyterian Church
Far Rockaway, New York, 1908

The somewhat severe exterior of this suburban church, designed in the New York office, belies its soaring interior. Mrs. Russell Sage gave the church as a memorial to her late husband, who made his fortune as a futures speculator and New York City's elevated railways king.

Cram's relationship with Mrs. Sage broke down entirely when, while Cram was out of the country, she chose to engage Louis Comfort Tiffany to design the great west win-dow. Cram had contemplated a twelve-lancet window de-picting the apostles and returned to find a secular Tiffany landscape installed. It was said that he never set foot inside the church again. Nevertheless, the church contains the largest Tiffany window in the world, unquestionably a mas-terpiece.

The construction is brick bearing walls with trim of cast-concrete faux limestone.

Interior of the south transept. Elaborate seating for presbyters behind the altar replaced the Catholic choir, and a masterfully carved pulpit is the focal point of abundant wood carving in the interior. (HDB/Cram & Ferguson Archive)

View of the west front showing the seven-part,
flamboyant Gothic window. (HDB/Cram &
Ferguson Archive; photo: Ethan Anthony)

St. Mary's Church
Walkerville, Ontario, 1908

This Anglican Church was built to serve the employees of a company town near Toronto built by the Hiram Walker Distillery. Architect Albert Kahn designed most of Walkerville in his interpretation of the International Style. Kahn preferred not to do the church because, as Cram wrote later, Kahn was Jewish and did not feel comfortable designing a Christian church. Thus he called on Cram for the design, and the Kahn office completed the construction documents. Cram combined elements of towers he had seen and photographed in England: the lower stages are quoted from All Saints' at Bray in Devon, the upper from parts of other towers from various colleges at Oxford University.

Exterior. (HDB/Cram & Ferguson Archive)

Interior of St. Mary's Church, incorporating tiles from the Moravian Pottery & Tile Works in Pennsylvania and woodcarvings by Johannes Kirchmeyer. (HDB/Cram & Ferguson Archive)

Cathedral of the Incarnation
Diocese of Baltimore, Maryland (project), 1908

Though only the Synod House was completed, the project for the Cathedral of the Incarnation is one illustration of the difference between the work of Goodhue and that of Cram. Two renderings show the design before and after the partners split.

Cram's roofs are steeply pitched; the clerestory walls are supported by flying buttresses, and the tower has large, prominent bell vents. The walls are more planar and delicate, and the stair towers ordered in a clear, formal hierarchy.

The Goodhue version, completed after the dissolution of the partnership, is far more modeled. The roof slopes have been reduced (some are flat), the walls are deeply carved, the windows occupy deeper wells in the wall, and many historical details, such as the pinnacles and perpendicular tracery, have disappeared. Gone are flying buttresses, replaced by massive buttresses and dramatic, thrusting stair towers. The tracery of the clerestory windows is bolder and heavier and the delicacy of the first scheme is replaced by a sculpted and more muscular quality overall.

Rendering, artist unknown, of Cram's design. (HDB/Cram & Ferguson Archive)

Rendering of the Cathedral of the Incarnation by Goodhue. (HDB/Cram & Ferguson Archive; photo: Peter A. Juley)

Church of the Ascension
Montgomery, Alabama, 1910

The Church of the Ascension is the first small church by Cram with a massive tower at the crossing, a feature he previously reserved for the larger churches. The form is largely based on St. Mary's at Iffley.

Exterior. (HDB/ Cram & Ferguson Archive; photo: Tebbs & Knell, Inc.)

Rendering. (Church of the Ascension)

Interior of the chancel of the Church of the Ascension.
(HDB/Cram & Ferguson Archive; photo: Tebbs & Knell, Inc.)

St. James Episcopal Church
New York, New York, 1911–24

St. James was designed by Henry Dudley in 1868. The tower in 1911 and the chancel, high altar, reredos and pulpit were designed in 1924 by Ralph Adams Cram and carved by the firm of Irving and Carson in Boston. Cram designed the new entrance on Madison Avenue. Most of the original stained glass windows were removed and replaced with new windows under Cram's direction. Many windows were made by Charles Connick, a frequent Cram collaborator.

Rendering of Cram's design for the new entrance and tower, artist unknown. (HDB/Cram & Ferguson Archive)

Rendering of Cram's design for the chancel of St. James Episcopal Church. (HDB/Cram & Ferguson Archive)

PROPOSED ALTERATIONS & ADDITIONS
SAINT JAMES CHURCH
NEW YORK CITY
CRAM & FERGUSON ARCHITECTS
248 BOYLSTON ST BOSTON MASS

Altar and reredos.
(HDB/Cram &
Ferguson Archive;
photo: Sigurd Fischer

St. Paul's Episcopal Church
Malden, Massachusetts, 1911

St. Paul's Malden is a charming scaled-down Whitby Abbey, though its tower was never completed. An early attempt at substituting cast stone for limestone, it is deteriorating badly and the exterior of the building is at risk.

Rendering by unknown artist of original scheme. (Courtesy St. Paul's Church)

West entry. (Photo: Ethan Anthony)

View of nave from balcony. (HDB/Cram & Ferguson Archive; photo: Paul J. Weber)

Drawing of Courage, one of the eight virtues that grace the altar front. (Courtesy Boston Public Library, Cram, Goodhue and Ferguson/Cram and Ferguson Collection)

Grace Episcopal Church Parish House
Manchester, New Hampshire, 1911

The roofline and treatment of the dormers bear a strong resemblance
to Edwin Lutyen's Deanery Garden house and to work by Mackay
Hugh Baillie Scott (1865–1945), the English Arts and Crafts architect.

Courtyard view. (HDB/Cram & Ferguson Archive)

House of Hope Presbyterian Church
St. Paul, Minnesota, 1916–26

This building was the personal gift of the Weyerhauser family to the Presbyterian community of St. Paul. The massing of the complex, with the smaller buildings nestling up to the church, shows the continuing influence of Goodhue in the firm's work.

Exterior view. (HDB/Cram & Ferguson Archive)

Fourth Presbyterian Church
Chicago, Illinois, 1912

Fourth Presbyterian combines a deeply recessed Gothic window with transverse porches. The west front has a decorated portico with a deep Gothic door. The attached parish buildings, designed under Cram's direction by Howard van Doren Shaw, successfully capture the Cram spirit and create a fine Gothic close.

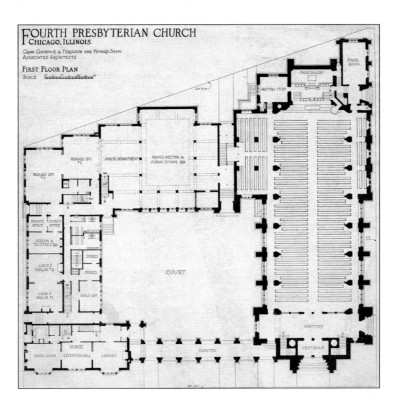

Plan. (HDB/Cram & Ferguson Archive)

The prominent buttresses along sides of the church foreshadow Cram's work on the nave at the Cathedral of St. John the Divine. (HDB/Cram & Ferguson Archive)

Detail of balcony over narthex with medieval-style beam work. (HDB/Cram & Ferguson Archive)

Detail of side altar. (HDB/Cram & Ferguson Archive)

Cloister. (HDB/Cram & Ferguson Archive)

Left: Balcony of Fourth Presbyterian Church. (HDB/Cram & Ferguson Archive)

Below left: View of nave with high gothic windows. (HDB/Cram & Ferguson Archive)

Below right: View of nave. (HDB/Cram & Ferguson Archive; photo: William H. Pierce & Co.)

Church of the New Jerusalem
Bryn Athyn, Pennsylvania, 1912

John Pitcairn, a wealthy Philadelphia merchant, commissioned Cram to build a Swedenborgian church using exclusively medieval construction methods. Oak timbers were cut from a nearby forest and seasoned in a local bog. Stone was quarried locally. For Cram, this was the realization of a dream; he wrote in "A Note on Bryn Athyn Church" in the *American Architect*, "By insensible degrees and in a short space of time, the idea of a sort of co-operative, neo-medieval organization for the building of the church, grew into dominance. . . . every new suggestion along these lines was welcomed, put in force and further developed, until at last, by the time the walls had begun to rise above the ground, the system had reached a point of development never achieved in any place since the close of the Middle Ages."

Unfortunately, the system was not wholly effective. As the design-construction process progressed, problems with Pitcairn's son, who tended to micromanage and compete with Cram, eventually induced Cram to step aside at the time work began on the tower.

Rendering by Cram. (From *Church Building*, 3rd ed. Boston: Small, Maynard & Co., 1914)

Tower of Church of the New Jerusalem as built. The elongation and exaggeration of the bell vent was introduced by Raymond Pitcairn Jr. (HDB/Cram & Ferguson Archive; photo: Paul J. Weber)

Photo taken during construction. (HDB/Cram & Ferguson Archive; photo: Paul J. Weber)

Side elevation showing Cram's dramatic massing. (HDB/Cram & Ferguson Archive; photo: Paul J. Weber)

West entry. (HDB/Cram & Ferguson Archive; photo: Paul J. Weber)

First Presbyterian Church
Oakland, California, 1912–13

First Presbyterian is one of several Cram churches that feature a western tower, square in plan with gables on all four facades, or with a gable whose axis is perpendicular to the axis of the nave. Similar churches include the 1908 St. Andrew's in Denver, and the 1930 project for the Blank Church in Chicago (see page 136).

Front elevation. (HDB/Cram & Ferguson Archive)

All Saints Episcopal Church
Peterborough, New Hampshire, 1913–21

All Saints was commissioned by Mrs. Walter Cheney Schofield, daughter of Benjamin Pierce Cheney, founder of American Express. Mrs. Schofeld was a generous benefactor of Peterborough, the original home of her grandfather, who was the town blacksmith. She was acquainted with Cram and his work through her husband, a professor of medieval studies at Harvard.

Exquisitely detailed, All Saints' is small and appropriately scaled for a New England village .

Six different finishes applied to the granite walls create an agreeably naturalized and varied texture. Inside and out, the church has a simple, rural aspect but also a high degree of refinement.

Front elevation. (HDB/Cram & Ferguson Archive)

Photograph of the donor, Mrs. Schofield, with Ralph Adams Cram at the dedication of All Saints Peterborough. (Courtesy All Saints')

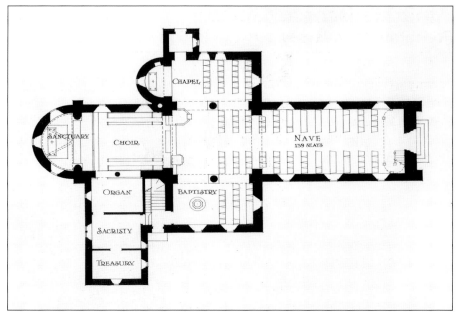

Plan of All Saints Episcopal Church. The plan and interior scheme of All Saints were taken almost literally from a village church in Iffley, England, a Romanesque design to which a Gothic chancel was added. (HDB/Cram & Ferguson Archive; photo: Arthur C. Haskell)

View toward altar. (HDB/ Cram & Ferguson Archive; photo: Paul J. Weber)

Trinity Episcopal Church
Princeton, New Jersey 1914 (addition)

Trinity was built in 1868 by Richard M. Upjohn, son of architect Richard Upjohn. Cram added a new chancel, furnishings, and altar. The Cram apse was modeled on the work of A. W. N. Pugin. It burned down in the 1960s.

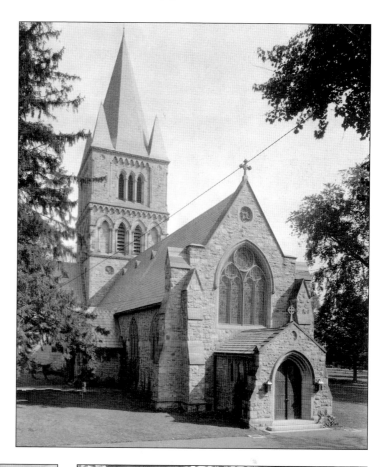

Right: Upjohn's Trinity Episcopal with Cram chancel. (HDB/Cram & Ferguson Archive; photo: Paul J. Weber)

Below left: Choir and chancel. (HDB/Cram & Ferguson Archive; photo: Paul J. Weber)

Below right: Altar and dossal curtain. (HDB/ Cram & Ferguson Archive; photo: Paul J. Weber)

Chapel for the Sisters of St. Anne
Arlington Heights, Massachusetts, 1914

Cram completed several commissions for the Sisters of St. Anne, an order of Anglican nuns, including a school in New York and this chapel for their school in Massachusetts. St. Anne's Chapel was Cram's idea of a chapel as a small farming village might build it: of simple local materials—whitewashed fieldstone gathered from the site, oak plank doors, slate roof, and hand-wrought hardware.

Exterior. (HDB/Cram & Ferguson Archive)

The interior. It included a monastic choir, a high altar, and a screen topped by a rude cross. The altar (shown here) and much of the interior were demolished to conform to the Vatican II liturgy. (HDB/Cram & Ferguson Archive; photo: Paul J. Weber)

St. Elizabeth Chapel at Whitehall
Sudbury, Massachusetts, 1914

Like the Chapel for the Sisters of St. Anne, built in the same year, Cram's family chapel at Whitehall, his country estate, was of fieldstone gathered from the property. The plan is simple, with a center aisle and an apsidal eastern end where a raised predella features an altar engaged in the east wall before a medieval Spanish triptych. On one side sat a small statue of St. Elizabeth of Hungary, namesake of the chapel and Bess Cram's favorite saint. Family friend Charles Connick provided the stained-glass rose and office artists designed the wrought-iron hardware made by noted craftsman Samuel Yellin. The Crams' daughter, Elizabeth, laid the final stone on the east wall. Mrs. Cram organized the worship services and outfitted the chapel with antiques, plate, and vestments gathered on the couple's trips around Europe and the Near East.

When the family was in residence, friends from the Cowley Fathers offered mass and neighbors were invited to attend. Services continued even after Cram's death.

The chapel today. Ralph Adams and Elizabeth Cram are buried here. (HDB/Cram & Ferguson Archive; photo: Ethan Anthony)

Cram at the door to his chapel. (HDB/Cram & Ferguson Archive)

Above left: Interior of St. Elizabeth Chapel. (HDB/ Cram & Ferguson Archive; photo: Paul J. Weber)

Above right: Chapel under construction. (HDB/ Cram & Ferguson Archive)

Cram family, clergy, and construction workers at the dedication of the chapel. (HDB/Cram & Ferguson Archive)

First Universalist Church
Somerville, Massachusetts, 1916

Cram sponsored the excavation of Cluny by Harvard professor Kenneth Conant. Reports of Conant's findings influenced this rare French Romanesque design by Cram. The church has been converted to a condominium development. (HDB/Cram & Ferguson Archive; photo: Paul J. Weber)

Sacred Heart Cathedral
Dodge City, Kansas, c. 1916

Here Cram reprised elements from Mexican-influenced work; it was said that he still competed with Goodhue after their split, and this may have encouraged his use of a style more widely associated with Goodhue. (HDB/Cram & Ferguson Archive)

Ellingwood Funerary Chapel
Nahant, Massachusetts, 1919

The Ellingwood Chapel is one of the Iffley series, as Peterborough was. This has a more planar quality that lends both a modern and a somber tone to the building. The austerity of the exterior suited the original use as a funeral chapel. The elegantly proportioned chapel with exposed wood beams creating a simple rhythm overhead is still used for concerts and social events. The gabled tower resembles contemporaneous work of Randall Wells (1877–1942), specifically the Church of St. Edward the Confessor at Kempley, Gloucestershire.

Exterior. (HDB/Cram & Ferguson Archive)

St. James Church
Lake Delaware, New York, 1920

Designed for Angelica Gerry, heir to a New York land fortune and descendant of Massachusetts governor Elbridge Gerry, St. James is a delicately spired gem organized around an auto court, another first for Cram.

A massive central tower and a broach roof spire distinguish St. James Church. ((HDB/Cram & Ferguson Archive; photo: Kevin Hogan)

Cram with Angelica Gerry, and members of the choir shortly after completion of the church. (Courtesy St. James Church)

Trinity Episcopal Church
Houston, Texas, 1920

William Ward Watkin, Cram's Houston office partner, collaborated with Cram on the design of Trinity Episcopal, later revised by Cram, whose changes were not recorded. Trinity was executed in smooth white Texas limestone.

Early view. (HDB/Cram & Ferguson Archive; photo: Tebbs-Kell, Inc.)

West door view.
(HDB/Cram & Ferguson
Archive; photo: Tebbs-
Knell, Inc.)

High altar of Texas lime-
stone. (HDB/Cram &
Ferguson Archive; photo:
Tebbs-Knell, Inc.)

Sacred Heart Church
Jersey City, New Jersey, 1921

A Gothic exterior conceals Cram's only Roman interior; great round columns and a vaulted chancel ceiling transport visitors to Cram's chancel, which is decorated with wrought-iron screens and colored marble. At this writing Sacred Heart is for sale. Having recently lost its Dominican clergy, the church's fate remains uncertain.

Exterior. (HDB/Cram & Ferguson Archive; photo: Paul J. Weber)

Nave, view toward entrance. (HDB/Cram & Ferguson Archive; photo: Sigurd Fischer)

Central Union Church
Honolulu, Hawaii, 1922

Cram was an advocate of classical (or what he called "colonial-based") styles for Protestant churches. Central Union allowed him to diverge from his customary Gothic to experiment with Wren-style elements. (HDB/Cram & Ferguson Archive; photo: Williams Studio)

The interior features classical columns with Corinthian capitals. Cram rarely used this style outside an academic setting. (HDB/Cram & Ferguson Archive; photo: Commercial & Photographic Co.)

First Presbyterian Church
Tacoma, Washington, 1923

With its Byzantine dome-topped tower and Venetian windows, First Presbyterian Tacoma is Cram's idealized vision of Hagia Sofia with English Gothic pinnacles. (HDB/Cram & Ferguson Archive)

The central tower houses a great Greek Cross plan. (HDB/Cram & Ferguson Archive)

View into the cloister showing banded brick- and stonework. (HDB/ Cram & Ferguson Archive)

Trinity Methodist Episcopal Church
Durham, North Carolina, 1923

A rare three-vent tower with a group of three windows reinforces the Trinity theme in an otherwise prototypical Cram urban neighborhood church.

Above: Rendering. (HDB/Cram & Ferguson Archive)

Above right: Detail of altar rail and pulpit. (HDB/Cram & Ferguson Archive; photo: Tebbs & Knell, Inc.)

Right: Early view of the church. The spire shown in the rendering was not built. (HDB/Cram & Ferguson Archive; photo: Tebbs & Knell, Inc.)

First Presbyterian Church
Jamestown, New York, 1923

A very large tower to accommodate a carillon reflects the carillon craze then sweeping the United States. The Romanesque tower reflects Cram's trip to Spain the year before. This church apparently was not built.

Rendering. (HDB/Cram & Ferguson Archive)

St. Paul's Episcopal Church
Yonkers, New York, 1924

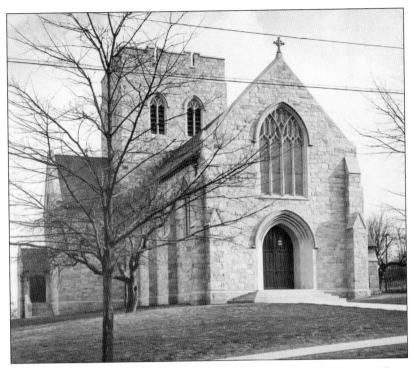

Above: A reprise of themes first applied at All Saints Peterborough (see page 97): a powerful central tower block, and the west front framed by massive buttresses with a single arch and deeply inset door. (HDB/Cram & Ferguson Archive)

Right: The interior also recalls that of All Saints', with less elaboration. (HDB/ Cram & Ferguson Archive)

National Presbyterian Church
Washington, DC, 1924 (project)

Model for a church that was never built. (HDB/Cram & Ferguson Archive; photo: Dadmun Co.)

Cathedral of St. John the Divine
New York, New York, 1925–31

Cram's contributions to St. John the Divine were completed in 1931, but the cathedral, one of the largest in the world, is still unfinished, so great is its scale and so complex its conception. As recounted in the introduction, Cram became consulting architect to the diocese in 1911 and took over work on the Gothic–Romanesque cathedral on the death of George Heins. Cram oversaw completion of the nave according to plans approved by the trustees in 1916.

St. John the Divine had no direct antecedents—it was larger than any Gothic structure ever built in Europe, but it resembled cathedrals of the French High Gothic. Its vast scale called for the massing of fortified French chateaus, as opposed to the more delicate designs of the English Perpendicular.

In the main crossing of St. John the Divine, Cram was faced with a much wider footprint than that of a Gothic interior. He "wove" pointed Gothic arches inside the previous Romanesque construction. The form creates a rigorously Gothic profile in a form and size without precedent.

Cram sponsored numerous stained-glass artists, notably Charles Connick, whose contributions continued throughout the twenty-year construction period. Other artists whose work Cram brought to the cathedral included sculptor John Evans and the creator of the golden doors, Henry Wilson.

Rendering, artist unknown, of Cram's scheme
for the exterior, as accepted by the trustees,
c. 1931. (HDB/Cram & Ferguson Archive;
photo: Rollin W. Bailey)

View of Cathedral of St. John the Divine from the east.
(HDB/Cram & Ferguson Archive)

Rendering of interior of nave. (HDB/Cram & Ferguson Archive)

St. Mary's Catholic Church
Detroit, Michigan, 1925

Although few Cram works are Romanesque, St. Mary's is one of his more memorable churches due to its exquisite proportions and composition and inventive placement of a Romanesque window where normally one would find a rose.

Early view of the church. (HDB/Cram & Ferguson Archive; photo: Thomas Ellison)

Emmanuel Church (project)
Rockford, Illinois, 1927

Rendering of exterior,
artist unknown. (HDB/
Cram & Ferguson
Archive)

Rendering of side aisle.
(HDB/Cram & Ferguson
Archive)

St. Paul's Church
Winston-Salem, North Carolina, 1927

This view of the church from below emphasizes its powerful massing and shows the influence of the modern trend toward streamlining in the firm's work. (HDB/Cram & Ferguson Archive)

American Church of Paris
Paris, France, 1927

This church on the banks of the Seine is one of Cram's masterpieces. The tower is placed on the front, where it becomes the entry feature. A riot of perpendicular Gothic detail—pinnacles, crochets, a grand spire (rare for Cram towers)—its lower story looks out onto a small courtyard that serves as a cloister element.

View of the tower. (HDB/Cram & Ferguson Archive; photo: Ethan Anthony)

Interior. ((HDB/Cram & Ferguson Archive; photo: Ethan Anthony)

St. Florian's Church
Detroit, Michigan, 1928

St. Florian's is an important Detroit church built by Polish immigrants. Cram extended and remodeled the original church, adding a powerful street front and rose window and an enlarged chancel.

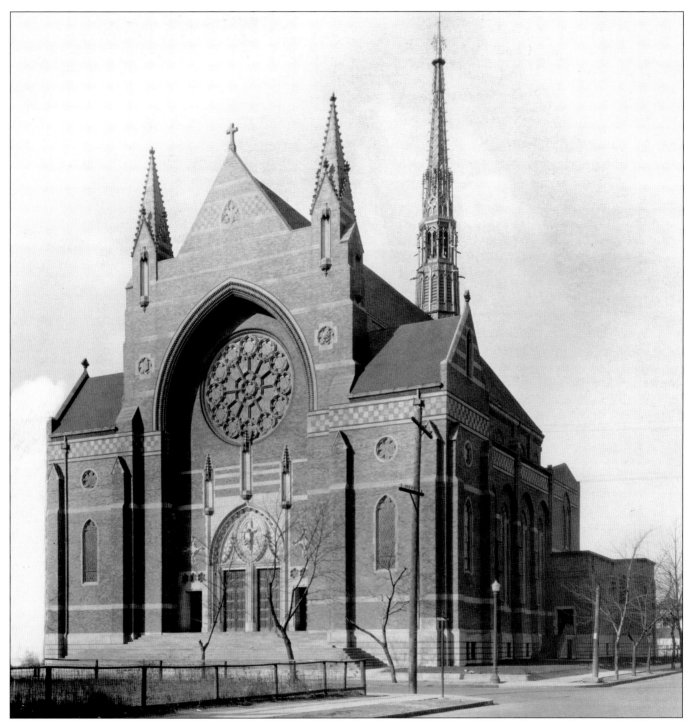

Early view of the exterior. (HDB/Cram & Ferguson Archive; photo: Thomas Ellison)

Interior of St. Florian's
Church. (HDB/Cram &
Ferguson Archive;
photo: Thomas Ellison)

Prince Memorial Chapel
Fort Meyer, Virginia, 1929 (project)

Planned memorial at Arlington
National Cemetery for the first
American aviator killed in
World War I. (HDB/Cram &
Ferguson Archive)

St. Vincent's Church
Los Angeles, California, 1927

St. Vincent's is based on late 18th-century Mexican ecclesiastical architecture, a variant of Spanish Baroque. The architect for the exterior was Albert C. Martin. Donors Edward and Estelle Doheny commissioned Cram to design parts of the interior including the chancel and baptistry.

Rendering. (HDB/Cram & Ferguson Archive; photo: R. M. Shaw)

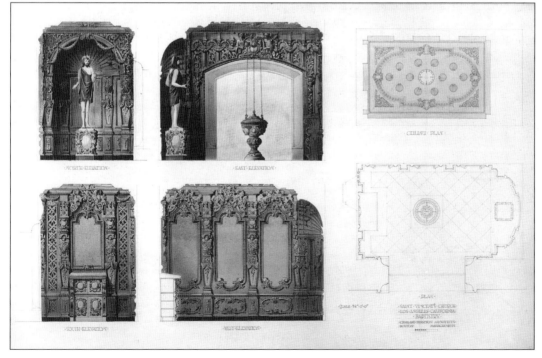

Rendering of baptistry design. (HDB/Cram & Ferguson Archive; photo: R. M. Shaw)

Chancel interior. (HDB/Cram & Ferguson Archive;
photo: The Mott Studios)

Christ Church–United Methodist Church
New York, New York, 1929

The Byzantine style, which Cram had rejected as inappropriate for a Christian church most vocally at the Cathedral of St. John the Divine, appears elegantly here on a tight site on New York's Park Avenue. The Venetian inspiration reprises themes Cram had explored at Rice University some twenty years earlier. Office legend had it that this church was Cram's response to Goodhue's similarly Byzantine St. Bartholomew's, located just one block away. The roof is barrel-vaulted and the exterior bears a resemblance to the blocky forms of Greek-cross churches such as Hagia Sophia.

Rendering, artist unknown. (HDB/Cram & Ferguson Archive; photo: R. M. Shaw)

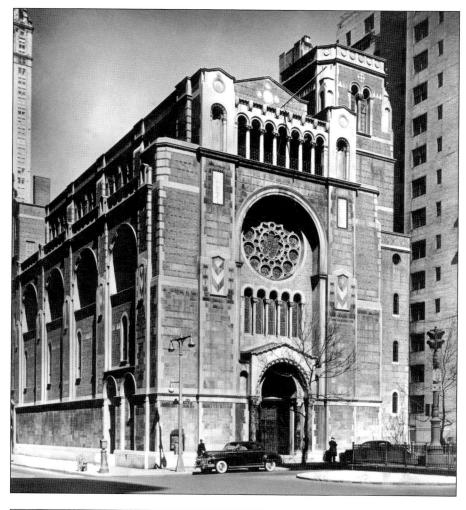

Early view. (HDB/
Cram & Ferguson
Archive)

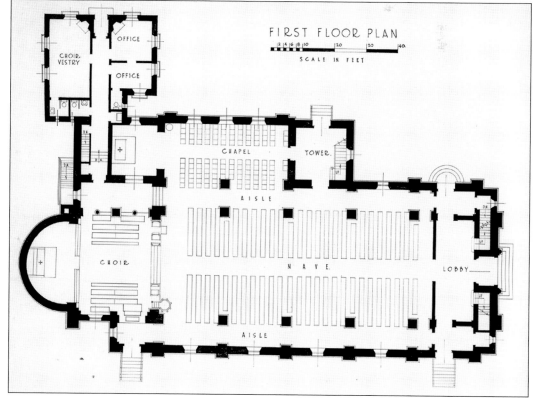

Plan. (HDB/Cram &
Ferguson Archive;
photo: R. M. Shaw)

All Saints Episcopal Church
Brookline, Massachusetts, c. 1929 (addition)

Rendering of church with parish house
addition, artist unknown. (HDB/Cram
& Ferguson Archive; photo: R. M. Shaw)

Klise Memorial Chapel East Congregational UCC Church
Grand Rapids, Michigan, 1929

Rendering, artist unknown, of unrealized full scheme: only the small chapel in the center was built. (HDB/Cram & Ferguson Archive)

Rendering, artist unknown, of cloister. (HDB/Cram & Ferguson Archive)

Interior view of Klise Memorial Chapel, toward entry. (HDB/Cram & Ferguson Archive)

Interior view, toward altar. (HDB/Cram & Ferguson Archive)

Mishawaka Cathedral
Mishawaka, Indiana, 1930 (project)

Rendering. (HDB/Cram & Ferguson Archive;
photo: R. M. Shaw)

East Liberty Presbyterian Church
Pittsburgh, Pennsylvania, 1931

Industrialist Andrew Mellon commissioned this church, but died before it was completed. When asked by his daughter-in-law if the design would be sufficiently Gothic to please the family, Cram replied that the church complex would be so unstintingly Gothic that Mrs. Mellon "would be unable to sleep nights," according to Chester Anderson Brown's undated manuscript, *My Best Years in* *Architecture with Ralph Adams Cram.* The church is cruciform in plan with a central lantern, and it possesses a sense of grandeur that belies its relatively modest size. Its exterior thrusts itself skyward with impressive spires and pinnacles. Its elaborate stonework was beautifully executed by John Evans, whose work Cram used at St. John the Divine, among other churches.

Early view of exterior. (HDB/Cram & Ferguson Archive, office reprint from *Architectural Forum*, undated)

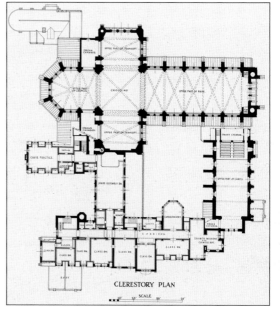

Plan. (HDB/Cram & Ferguson Archive)

Interior. (HDB/Cram & Ferguson Archive)

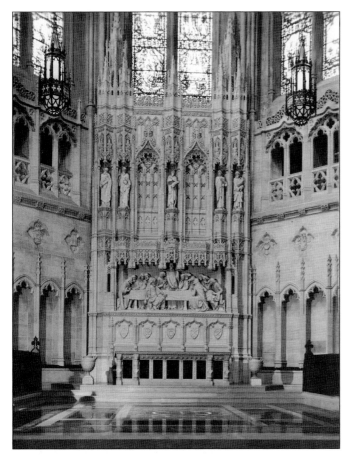

High altar of East Liberty Presbyterian Church. (HDB/Cram & Ferguson Archive; photo: Arthur C. Haskell)

View of nave. (HDB/Cram & Ferguson Archive; photo: Arthur C. Haskell)

Sketch, dated 1933, for relief of the Last Supper over the altar. (HDB/Cram & Ferguson Archive; photo: John Angel)

John Evans (center) at work on sculpture. (HDB/Cram & Ferguson Archive; photo: George Brown & Co.)

Baptismal font tower. (HDB/Cram & Ferguson Archive; photo: Irving & Casson, A. H. Davenport Co.)

Second Unitarian Church
Boston, Massachusetts, 1934

Like Central Union in Honolulu, this is a classical-style church. It was probably the work of partners Chester Godfrey or Alexander Hoyle.

Exterior. (HDB/Cram & Ferguson Archive; Photo: Paul J. Weber)

Interior. (HDB/Cram & Ferguson Archive; photo: Paul J. Weber)

Blank Church
Chicago, Illinois, 1935 (project)

Rendering, artist unknown, for an unrealized church with a rectangular tower terminated by gables and a fleche. Compare St. Andrew's, Denver, and Oakland First Presbyterian. (HDB/Cram & Ferguson Archive)

Conventual Church of Sts. Mary and John
Cambridge, Massachusetts, 1936

Funded by Isabella Stewart Gardner, prominent Boston philanthropist, this church with a Norman interior and Romanesque exterior was for the Cowley Fathers Monastery (also designed by Cram). The exquisite small chapel is clad inside and out with granite. It won the Boston Society of Architects' 1936 Harleston Parker prize for the most beautiful building of the year.

Entry facade. (HDB/Cram & Ferguson Archive; photo: Arthur C. Haskell)

Interior. (HDB/Cram & Ferguson Archive; photo: Arthur C. Haskell)

All Saints Episcopal Church
Winter Park, Florida, 1938

In part because of his age (he was 75), Cram had a limited role in this design, which was handled by partner Chester Brown. Cram was disappointed that his preference for Spanish Colonial, which he considered as appropriate for Florida, was toned down considerably for cost reasons. The result was a small modern church of Gothic inspiration.

Exterior. (HDB/Cram & Ferguson Archive)

Rendering, artist unknown, of interior. (HDB/Cram & Ferguson Archive)

St. Thomas Church
Peoria, Illinois, 1939

St. Thomas, like All Saints, Winter Park (opposite page) represents a common thread of smaller, more spartan designs produced before the war. The employment of plaster vaults, a device Cram deplored as cheap, signals Cram's waning influence. Plaster vaulted ceiling, simple masonry walls, and modern stained glass belie Cram's participation in this late design.

Front. (HDB/Cram & Ferguson Archive; photo: Frank Oberkoetter Studios)

Interior. (HDB/Cram & Ferguson Archive; photo: Frank Oberkoetter Studios)

3. Academic Architecture

Though Cram is known for his religious work, his career really began with his win of the West Point competition, a project that, appropriately for him, included both religious and academic structures (medieval monks had developed the first institutions of higher education).

After Princeton's president Woodrow Wilson chose Cram to design the master plan for the university, Cram became the preeminent campus planner in the country, leading to commissions at a range of institutions unequaled by any other architect or firm then or since. These commissions include: eleven buildings at Williams College; seven each at Rice University, Wheaton College, Sweet Briar College, and the University of Richmond; three at Princeton and Boston University; one each at Notre Dame, Wellesley, Rollins, and Hamilton, and the Class of 1908 gate to Harvard Yard. Cram's secondary school buildings are at Phillips Exeter Academy (eighteen buildings); St. Paul's, Choate, Taft, Miss Masters, Kent, St. George's, and Mercersburg, among others.

From the first academic project he designed (the master plan for Wheaton College) to the last (the library at the University of Southern California at Los Angeles), the academic architecture of Ralph Adams Cram features ample, flawlessly crafted, user-oriented spaces. Organization is straightforward, circulation simple and understandable, decoration always tastefully understated in rich, well-detailed materials. Whether nominally Gothic, Spanish Colonial, Georgian, or Byzantine, the buildings are fine and full of character.

In the earlier buildings like those at Wheaton, with budgets low and aspirations high, elegant details are used sparingly. In later, more amply funded projects such as the Graduate College at Princeton or the chapel at St. George's, detail is abundant to the point of extravagance. Window seats and carved details provide a joyful reminder to the passerby that once someone thought very deeply about the experience of being in that place long into the future. The spiritual and physical welfare of the whole person was Cram's guiding light. Today, the students who use the buildings—some lovingly preserved for over a hundred years—still delight in observing these small signs of the enduring traditions in which they hope to eventually take their own place.

Wheaton College
Norton, Massachusetts, 1898–1932

In 1898 Samuel Cole, then president of Wheaton Women's Seminary, asked Cram to design a master plan for the expansion of the Wheaton Seminary for women. The school had just twenty-five students and Cram's master plan for the campus began with a modest sketch on a scrap of paper. Cram envisioned a central quadrangle at the highest point of the land he dubbed the Court of Honor, a rectangular space headed by a library and lined along its long axis by ranks of neo-Georgian buildings. The firm's first building at Wheaton was dedicated three years later. Chapin Hall, a severe colonial brick dormitory, housed the entire student body of seventy-five.

The firm worked at Wheaton from 1911 to 1932 on buildings for the science and administration departments, three more dormitories, and the library, bringing the total to seven buildings. The first administration building at the college, Park Hall (c. 1932) has an almost spartan Georgian brick exterior reflecting the modest budget for most of the buildings on the Wheaton campus, yet the interior ceiling features a graceful barrel vault surmounted by a round lantern, similar to contemporary work of Webb and Shaw (see figs. I-35 and I-36, page 32). Most of the Wheaton buildings were designed by Cram associates, under the guidance of partners Alexander Hoyle and John Doran. The buildings are characterized by symmetrical plans; they are clad in red brick trimmed in Indiana limestone. Palladian windows accent the otherwise restrained facades and low-sloped roofs are capped with white painted wooden balustrades. Today, Cram's Court of Honor endures, though the students call it the "dimple" for the glacial kettle in the middle that was never filled.

Wallace Library, 1916.

Wallace Library is the culmination of Cram's 1898 master plan and heads the quad with a Beaux-Arts design that arguably employs the architecture he and Goodhue had fought against twenty years earlier in winning the West Point competition. The Wheaton design appears also to draw from Trumbauer's 1915 Widener Library at Harvard, itself a product of the École, through Trumbauer's head draftsman Julian Abele. (HDB/Cram & Ferguson Archive; photo: Paul J. Weber, 1948)

Cole Memorial Chapel, 1915.

The firm's work at Wheaton grew more elaborate as time passed. Cole Memorial Chapel combines a Wren-like steeple and a Corinthian temple front.

Left: exterior. (HDB/Cram & Ferguson Archive; photo: Paul J. Weber)

Below: interior (HDB/Cram & Ferguson Archive; photo: Arthur C. Haskell)

Kilham Hall, 1931.

Kilham Hall bears a resemblance to Eltham Lodge, an English Renaissance country house designed in 1664 by Hugh May, a follower of Inigo Jones and colleague of Christopher Wren. The parti is a colonnaded central pavilion terminated at each end by symmetrical blocks of rooms. (HDB/Cram & Ferguson Archive; photo: R. M. Shaw)

Sweet Briar College
Sweet Briar, Virginia, 1902–66

Sweet Briar College was founded in 1900 with the gift of Indiana Fletcher of part of her family's land in southwestern Virginia. In 1901 the Board of Trustees commissioned Cram, Goodhue and Ferguson to design a master plan. An entirely new campus for the college was to be built on 3,300 acres of the 8,000-acre former plantation near Lynchburg. Cram and Goodhue tried to persuade the college to allow them to employ the Gothic style, but the trustees insisted the buildings be designed in a vernacular Virginia style. Though he did not mention it, Cram certainly would have been familiar with Jefferson's University of Virginia, and early schemes for Sweet Briar feature a colonnaded lower floor around a green quadrangle similar in concept to the Virginia campus. The eventual plan proposed by Cram and Goodhue (who drew all of the renderings) included a quadrangle of imposing geometric parterres on the summit of the hill, closed on three sides and open on the downhill side to views of the valley below. Years of financial problems prevented the completion of the grand scheme; utilitarian buildings added in recent years have rendered the campus most notable for its lost promise.

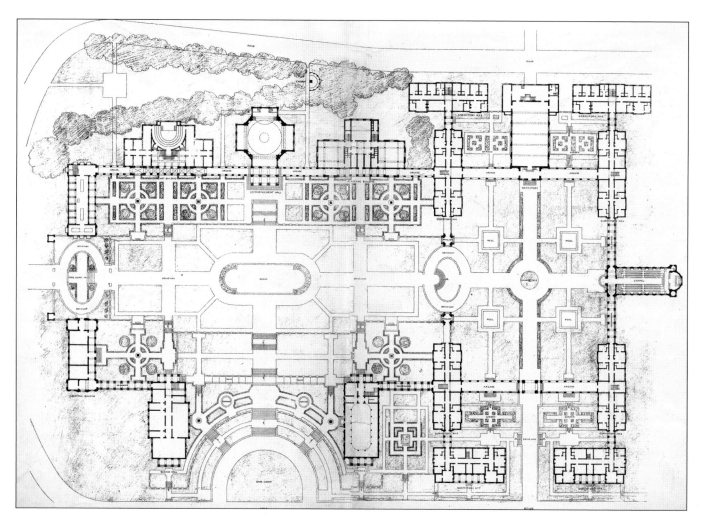

Proposed campus plan, 1902.

The effect Cram intended was an English acropolis of learning which in this case was to grow up from the ashes of the old South. Goodhue's extraordinary rendering of the master plan featured two symmetrical axes, one to be headed by a Commencement Hall similar to Jefferson's Rotunda in Charlottesville, the other by an imposing Georgian chapel. Neither was realized. (HDB/Cram & Ferguson Archive)

Perspectives by Bertram Goodhue.

These sketches show the intention to use monumental architecture to frame views of the fields below and the Chapel to the east (*top*) and the Sweet Briar bell tower (*center*), one of the few landscape elements realized as imagined by the firm. (HDB/Cram & Ferguson Archive, office reprints from *American Architect*, August 23, 1902, and August 30, 1902)

Fletcher Hall, 1924.

Fletcher Hall incorporates a fragment of the arcade that Cram envisioned to connect all buildings of the quadrangle. Though attempted several times, the arcade element was never fully realized in the firm's academic work. (HDB/Cram & Ferguson Archive; photo: Paul J. Weber)

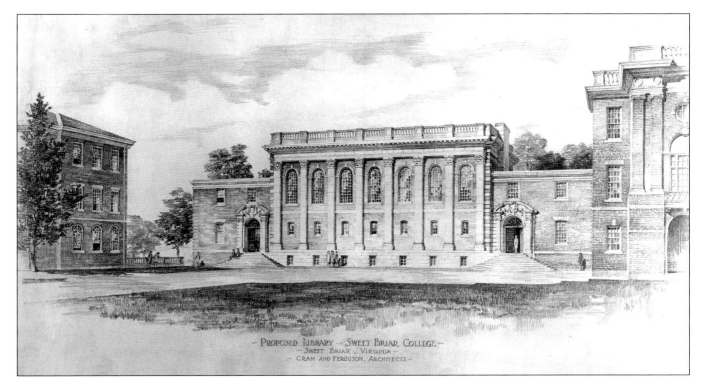

PROPOSED LIBRARY · SWEET BRIAR COLLEGE ·
· SWEET BRIAR · VIRGINIA ·
· CRAM AND FERGUSON, ARCHITECTS ·

Mary Cochran Library, 1927.

Above: The raised classical porch was reinterpreted as a central element with monumental pilasters, a theme explored at Wheaton and revisited in the 1922 Stetson Library at Williams College (see page 173). (HDB/Cram & Ferguson Archive; photo: R. M. Shaw)

Left: View of a typical walk in the romantic garden as rendered by Goodhue. (Courtesy of Austin Cribben)

Proposed chapel, 1936.

Top: Rendering, artist unknown. The chapel was sited at the head of the garden in the place where Jefferson had sited his library at the University of Virginia. (HDB/ Cram & Ferguson Archive)

Bottom: Rendering, artist unknown. Chapel interior. (HDB/Cram & Ferguson Archive)

United States Military Academy
West Point, New York, 1904–1923

As recounted in the introduction, in 1902 Cram's firm was invited to participate in a competition for the design of a new master plan and a number of buildings for the U. S. Military Academy at West Point. In the architectural community the competition was viewed, as Cram noted in his autobiography, as a "battle of styles" between Gothic and Beaux-Arts classicism. When the Gothic scheme of Cram and Goodhue was selected, the classicists complained that American architecture would be set back a quarter century, but more disinterested critics were pleased. The campus already had a Gothic revival chapel dating to the 1850s, and some architects felt that Gothic style was more adaptable to modern conditions than the École's classicism.

The firm was required by the government to open a second office in New York to manage the West Point commission, and Goodhue, who had been in New York during his apprenticeship, chose to move there to head the office. The first buildings executed were the Post Headquarters, designed in Boston under the direction of Cram, and the Cadet Chapel (1904–6), overseen by Goodhue in New York. Both combine elements of medieval crenellated architecture in the military style that recalls the French fortress monastery of Mont Saint Michel. To Cram the medieval citadel was a symbol of a high point of chivalric culture, with Church and State united as more or less equal partners in government.

Aerial view of the Academy after completion of the chapel and Post headquarters buildings. (HDB/Cram & Ferguson Archive)

Main Gate of the United States Military Academy.

This rendering, date unknown, by Goodhue includes ornamentation probably based on books of measured drawings of medieval English buildings, such as those by A. W. N. Pugin, Viollet-le-Duc, and others. The firm library contained hundreds of such books. (HDB/Cram & Ferguson Archive)

A GATEWAY, UNITED STATES MILITARY ACADEMY, WEST POINT, NEW YORK (C. G. & F.)

Drawn by Mr. Goodhue

Cadet Chapel, 1904

View from the east. The site of the Cadet Chapel, on the highest plateau of the campus, makes it the crowning feature of the plan. Its solid massing, even with a clerestory wall that is "skeletonized to the utmost," as the critic Montgomery Schuyler observed, creates a commanding presence over the campus. The Gothic design for the chapel was controversial, some at the Academy believing that religious elements, such as the monastic choir, were inappropriate for a public institution. Despite these dissenting views, broad support mobilized in support of Goodhue's plan and it was carried out unchanged. (HDB/Cram & Ferguson Archive; photo: Paul J. Weber)

View of Cadet Chapel from the west.
(HDB/Cram & Ferguson Archive;
photo: Paul J. Weber)

Interior of the Cadet Chapel.
(HDB/Cram & Ferguson Archive;
photo: Paul J. Weber)

Post Headquarters, 1904.

The grounding of Cram's design in a polemic argument is evident in the Post Headquarters. To promote the medieval code of chivalry as a model of behavior for the American army office, he used the architectural language of ramparts, crenellations, and sally port, recalling the Christian kingdoms—his ideal of a moral and aristocratic society. The interior of the building is more open and ornamental than the implacable exterior, with heraldic coat-of-arms designed by Cram to symbolize the states and territories of the United States.

Right: Side view. (HDB/Cram & Ferguson Archive; photo: Paul J. Weber)

Below: Main entry. (HDB/Cram & Ferguson Archive; photo: Paul J. Weber)

Princeton University,
Princeton, New Jersey, 1906–29

In 1906 Woodrow Wilson, then president of the university, appointed Cram as consulting architect to Princeton. At that time, Cram characterized the campus as a "pleasure park," conjuring the image of a theme-park collection of buildings, each designed to please the stylistic preferences of its individual donor. Wilson hoped to bring more order to the planning and transform Princeton into a model American intellectual center. He planned to do this by conceptually and physically modeling it on Oxford University, in his and Cram's view the highest development of the English university. Cram began by proposing to fit all new buildings into his new homogeneous and integrated campus plan. Individual buildings would be inspired by Gothic precedents, tendencies of the donors notwithstanding. Earlier Gothic revival buildings had been completed on the campus by architects Day and Klauder and Cope and Stewardson, but Cram's master plan moved and demolished buildings and inserted new ones at strategic points to create new exterior spaces. Princeton's Collegiate Gothic soon became the model for many other American colleges and universities.

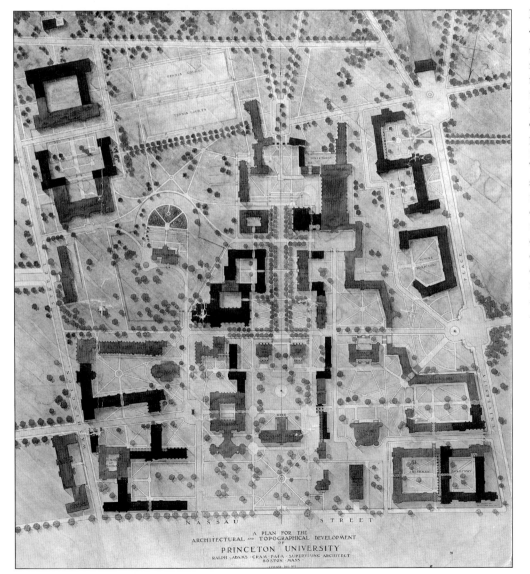

Master Plan, 1907–22.

The master plan emerged from the existing symmetry of Cannon Green, a new central space for a campus that lacked a central quadrangle. Cram's placement of other new buildings created a hierarchy of smaller, partially enclosed courts in a delicate interplay of axis and edge. The sense of enclosure of these spaces contrasts with openings that reveal new vistas. This use of multiple possibilities, allowing the user to complete the space conceptually, became a hallmark of Cram's campus planning in contrast to the axial and symmetrical plans of the Beaux-Arts. (HDB/Cram & Ferguson Archive)

Campbell Hall, 1909.

This dormitory established several aspects of what became the classic collegiate Gothic style, including a plan based on pairs of bedrooms sharing a common study and fireplace. The arrangement recalls the student rooms around the lawn at the University of Virginia.

Above: View from lawn, 1992. (HDB/Cram & Ferguson Archive; photo: Ethan Anthony)

Right: Detail of stone work, 1992. (HDB/Cram & Ferguson Archive; photo: Ethan Anthony)

Campbell Hall, 1909.

Above: Perspective rendering. (HDB/Cram & Ferguson Archive)

Below: Exterior. (HDB/Cram & Ferguson Archive; photo: Sigurd Fischer)

Graduate College, 1913.

As one of Cram's most highly developed academic buildings, the Graduate College employs studied irregularity, a picturesque exterior, and a succession of visual surprises inside. The building achieves Ruskinian ideals of craftsmanship in the stone work, restraint in its ornament, and a few spaces, such as the Great Hall of the refectory, of impressive drama.

Right: Plan. (HDB/Cram & Ferguson Archive)

Below left: General view. (HDB/Cram & Ferguson Archive)

Below right: Cleveland Tower. (HDB/Cram & Ferguson Archive)

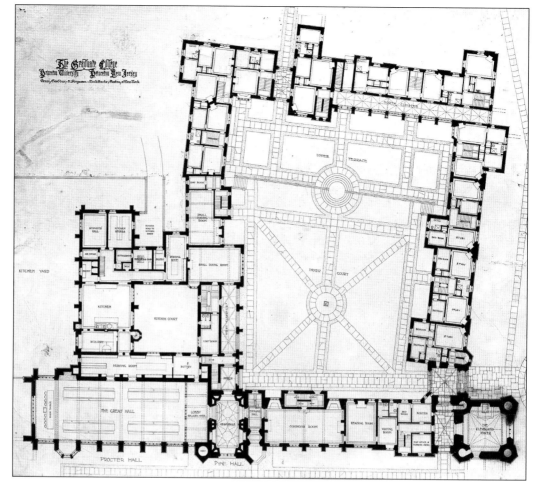

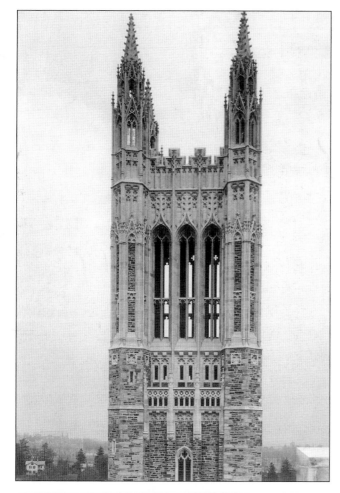

Left: Detail of Graduate College tower
(HDB/Cram & Ferguson Archive)

Below left: Interior of refectory.
(HDB/Cram & Ferguson Archive; photo:
Paul J. Weber)

Below right: Detail and ceiling woodwork
(HDB/Cram & Ferguson Archive)

McCormick Hall, 1922.

The architecture building in its original incarnation was Arts and Crafts Byzantine with Mexican overtones. Subsequent overbuilding and clumsy renovations and additions have rendered the architecture building and Cram's original master plan unrecognizable.

Above: Exterior. (HDB/Cram & Ferguson Archive)

Below: Presentation drawing of elevation. (HDB/Cram & Ferguson Archive, office reprint from *Architecture*, Nov. 1923, Pl. CLXII)

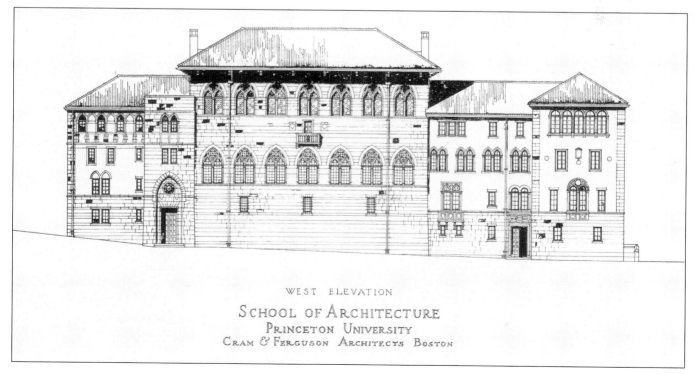

WEST ELEVATION

SCHOOL OF ARCHITECTURE
PRINCETON UNIVERSITY
CRAM & FERGUSON ARCHITECTS BOSTON

Interior of McCormick Hall. (HDB/Cram & Ferguson Archive; photo: Mattie P. Hewitt)

University Chapel, 1920–28.

Exterior. (HDB/Cram & Ferguson Archive)

John Grier Hibben, a Presbyterian minister, who succeeded Woodrow Wilson as president of Princeton (1912–32), commissioned Cram to design a new chapel when the existing chapel was destroyed by fire. Hibben and Cram were of one mind in wanting to emphasize religious life in the university. Cram wrote that the design should strike "some workable balance between archeology and creative art." The eventual interior design, primarily by Cram with the assistance of Alexander Hoyle, was modeled after English collegiate chapels at Oxford and Cambridge. The exterior, contemporaneous with work at the Cathedral of St. John the Divine, marked Cram's turn from English to French Gothic.

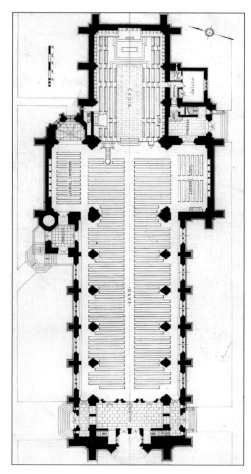

University Chapel.

Above: Plan. (HDB/Cram & Ferguson Archive; photo: William H. Pierce Co.)

Above right: Rendering of chapel, artist unknown. (HDB/Cram & Ferguson Archive)

Rothschild Memorial Rothschild Arch, rendering, 1929.

Cram's last work at Princeton was the design of this entrance to the campus. Arguments with a new administration over control of the design led Cram to resign the position of Campus Architect. (HDB/Cram & Ferguson Archive; photo: R. M. Shaw)

Rice Institute (now Rice University)
Houston, Texas, 1908–57

Shortly after his appointment as Consulting Architect at Princeton, Cram received a letter from Dr. Edgar Lovett, the president of the newly formed Rice Institute, inviting him to indicate his interest in designing a campus for the Institute. Lovett, a former Princeton professor, had recently been appointed president of the Institute, formed under the legacy of a murdered Houston cotton and timber baron, William Marsh Rice.

In 1909 Cram, Goodhue and Ferguson submitted three different campus plans. The trustees approved Plan C, which incorporated elements of the master planning work Cram had begun at Princeton, particularly the emphasis on multiple interpretations of space as well as the Arts and Crafts Byzantine style based on Cram's fascination with the melding of Christian design with Islamic influences that he had seen on visits to Venice.

Work at Rice Institute proceeded at such a pace that the firm opened an office in Houston around 1911. It was headed by William Ward Watkin until 1919, when wartime rationing slowed construction of the campus. Watkin, who had been sent to Houston in 1910 as the on-site representative, founded the architecture program at Rice and continued to practice independently after the firm closed its office in 1922. He occasionally served as Cram and Ferguson's architect-in-charge for work in Houston throughout the 1920s.

Aerial view of campus, date unknown. (Photo: Courtesy 36th Division Aviation, Texas National Guard)

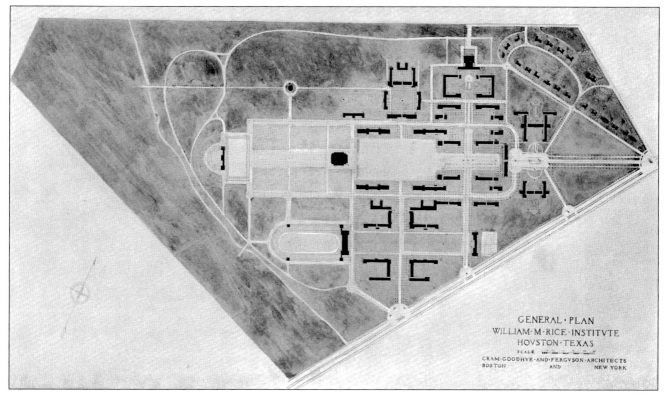

Rice Institute, Master Plan, 1909. (HDB/Cram & Ferguson Archive, office reprint from *American Architect*, Dec. 11, 1912)

Lovett Hall, 1912.

Main entry view of the administration building, which draws its stylistic direction and its massing from the Hagia Sophia in Istanbul. The architectural language juxtaposes richly carved Hellenistic and Justinian capitals and large planes of decorative patterned masonry. (HDB/Cram & Ferguson Archive: photo: E. W. Irish Photo Co.)

Side view of Lovett Hall. (HDB/Cram & Ferguson Archive)

Detail of column, Lovett Hall. (HDB/Cram & Ferguson Archive; photo: E. W. Irish Photo Co.)

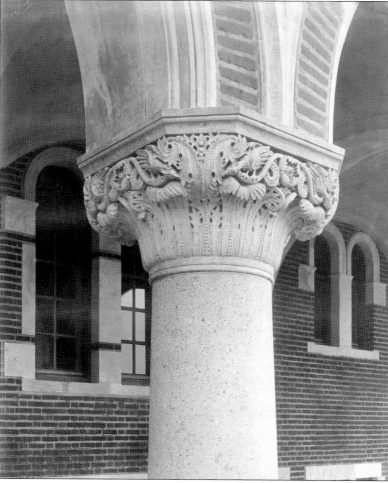

Cram at the dedication of Lovett Hall, in the back row of dignitaries, wearing a mortarboard. The academic recognition and degrees he never earned as a youth were bestowed upon him repeatedly as an adult. (HDB/Cram & Ferguson Archive)

Mechanical Engineering Laboratory and Power Plant, 1912.

The deep arcades that dominate the Rice plan were well suited to the hot Houston sun. (HDB/Cram & Ferguson Archive; photo: Tebbs & Knell Inc.)

Physics Lab 1914.

Top: General view. (HDB/Cram & Ferguson Archive)

Bottom: Front view. (HDB/Cram & Ferguson Archive)

Westhampton College, University of Richmond
Richmond, Virginia, 1910–16

In 1910, under the direction of the college president Reverend Dr. Frederic W. Boatwright, trustees of the University of Richmond resolved to move the institution from the city to the site of a former amusement park in the nearby suburbs of Richmond. Boatwright traveled to Boston to ask Cram to help him plan the new campus; he had studied Cram's work at Princeton and Rice, had read many of his books, and shared his passion for building an American Christian educational culture. The result was Westhampton, a women's college on the campus opened in 1914, where Cram's original six buildings established the Goth-

ic style of all but one of the school's future buildings. The palette of materials, like that at the contemporary Miss Masters and Taft Schools, is largely red brick and limestone trim; the design is based on stone buildings at Oxford University. Arts and Crafts tiles and abundant carved figures decorate the exterior, a new development for the firm. Gargoyles and bas-relief statues depict Boatwright, Cram, and other campus figures. Since 1916, the date of Cram's last work there, the university largely has required architects to copy Cram's style down to the smallest details.

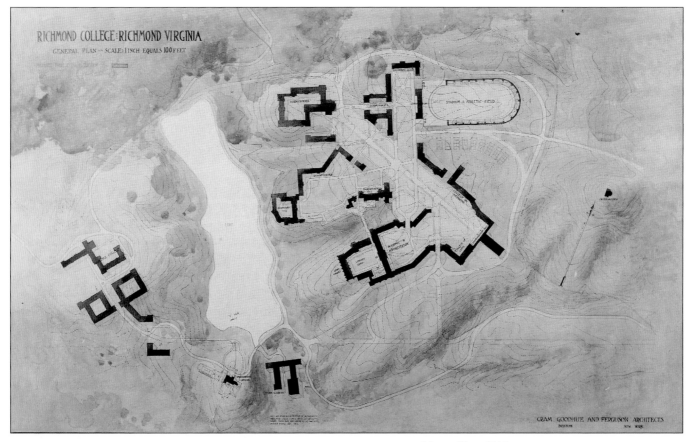

Master Plan, 1910.

Characteristically, Cram sought the highest point of the campus as his site for Westhampton College. His cloistered citadel crowns the hill, affording expansive views across the lake toward the main campus. (HDB/Cram & Ferguson Archive; photo: Dadum Co.)

Richmond College.

View of North Court from lawn.
(HDB/Cram & Ferguson
Archive)

North Court, courtyard view.
(HDB/Cram & Ferguson
Archive; photo: Paul J. Weber)

St. Mary's School
Peekskill, New York 1911

St. Mary's was originally designed as a seminary school run by an order of Episcopal nuns. Now reduced and converted into residential housing, it is the earliest Cram and Goodhue preparatory school building. Its Tudor style recalls other Tudor academic work the pair designed at the same time, for example, at the University of Richmond.

St. Mary's. (HDB/Cram & Ferguson Archive; photo: Bruce Richards)

Phillips Exeter Academy
Exeter, New Hampshire 1911–37

Work at Exeter—Cram's father's alma mater—began in 1911, with a master plan and design for Webster Hall. Ultimately, the firm designed a total of nineteen buildings more noteworthy for their perfection than for their originality. Most of the themes here are familiar if more perfectly executed neo-Georgian than at other Cram campuses.

The Exeter church is shown on page 48.

Academy Building entry. (HDB/Cram & Ferguson Archive; photo: Paul J. Weber)

The Academy Building at Phillips Exeter Academy, 1914, with its distinctive ship weathervane, conveys the dominance, conservatism and tradition of the Northeastern elite. The most distinguished elements of this building are its rich millwork and the English Renaissance ornamentation of the interior. (HDB/Cram & Ferguson Archive; photo: Arthur C. Haskell, 1950)

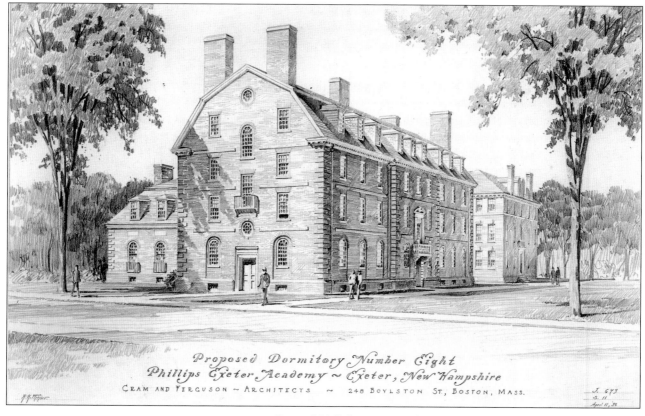

Proposed Dormitory Number Eight
Phillips Exeter Academy ~ Exeter, New Hampshire
CRAM AND FERGUSON ~ ARCHITECTS ~ 248 BOYLSTON ST, BOSTON, MASS.

Bancroft Hall dormitory, rendering by R. K. Fletcher. (HDB/Cram & Ferguson Archive; photo: R. M Shaw)

Wheelwright Hall dormitory. (HDB/Cram & Ferguson Archive; photo: Arthur C. Haskell)

Cilley Hall dormitory. (HDB/Cram & Ferguson Archive; photo: Paul J. Weber)

Williams College,
Williamstown, Massachusetts, 1912–38

At Williams, Cram realized his grand vision on a larger scale than he had achieved at Wheaton and Sweet Briar. Work began with the neo-Georgian Williams and Chapin Halls, both developed by Alexander Hoyle. Constructed in the characteristic office palette of brick trimmed in buff Indiana limestone, both buildings incorporate references to the English Renaissance and owe a debt to the contemporary work of Richard Norman Shaw. Despite Cram's stated preference for the Gothic, the Williams buildings are primarily Colonial style, with great attention to detail. Grand columned porticos recall temples of knowledge Cram had envisioned but never realized at Sweet Briar. Rooftop balustrades are carved in limestone here; on Wheaton and Sweet Briar's more modest budgets, they had been executed in wood.

Chapin Hall, 1912.

An English Renaissance portico marks the entrance to this 1,100-seat hall.

Left: Front view. (HDB/Cram & Ferguson Archive; photo: Paul J. Weber)

Below: Side view. (HDB/Cram & Ferguson Archive)

Stetson Library, 1922.

The most overtly English Arts and Crafts-inspired work at Williams is Stetson. The Palladian temple front is fully recessed in the facade, forming a classical raised porch similar to that planned for the Sweet Briar library (see page 146). Stetson served for thirty years as a faculty club, but the college plans to restore the library to this fine Hoyle design.

Above: Exterior. (HDB/Cram & Ferguson Archive)

Right: Interior. (HDB/Cram & Ferguson Archive; photo: Paul J. Weber)

Adams Memorial Theater, 1938.

The entrance portico of the theater at Williams
suggests classic Colonial architecture, a reference
to the college's revolutionary-era founding.
(HDB/Cram & Ferguson Archive; photo: Arthur
C. Haskell)

Mercersburg Academy
Mercersburg, Pennsylvania, 1916–26

The Mercersburg Chapel is a spired Gothic fortress at the center of the campus. (HDB/Cram & Ferguson Archive; photo: Paul J. Weber)

Mercersburg Chapel nave.
(HDB/Cram & Ferguson
Archive; photo: Paul J.
Weber)

View of nave from the altar.
(HDB/Cram & Ferguson
Archive)

The Masters School
Dobbs Ferry, New York, 1919

Three views of the building.

Top: Rugged massing recalls Parish Houses for Newton churches. (HDB/Cram & Ferguson Archive; photo: Paul J. Weber)

Center: Main entry facade. (HDB/Cram & Ferguson Archive)

Bottom: The tower element anchors lower buildings in the quad. (HDB/Cram & Ferguson Archive)

Tsuda University,
Hokkaido, Japan, c. 1919

The only academic project that Cram designed outside the United States, the master plan and building designs at Tsuda University blended elements of a monastic layout with details ranging from Japanese culture to modernism.

Founder Umeko Tsuda had lived in America as a girl. She attended Bryn Mawr College. When, before the turn of the century, she returned to Japan, she was dismayed at the treatment of women in her native country. Following her graduation from college, she resolved to dedicate herself to raising the status of Japanese women through education. Tsuda University became one of Japan's first Christian universities, an idea that naturally would have appealed to Cram.

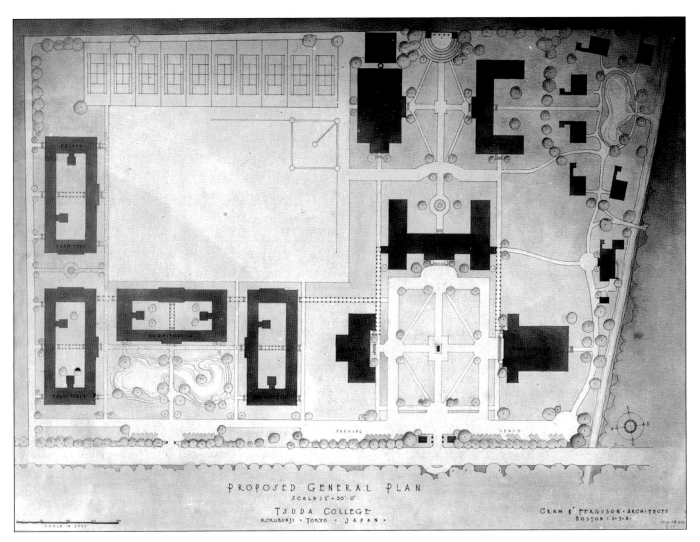

Master plan, 1919.

The master plan shows a simple organization of two main axes, with the administration building sitting squarely across the vertical axis. Buildings are arranged to create cloister-like courtyard spaces, two of which can be seen to be opposites: the upper symbolizes the delicate female geisha, the lower, the bulky male samurai. This abstract use of symbolism is uncharacteristic in Cram's architecture. (HDB/Cram & Ferguson Archive)

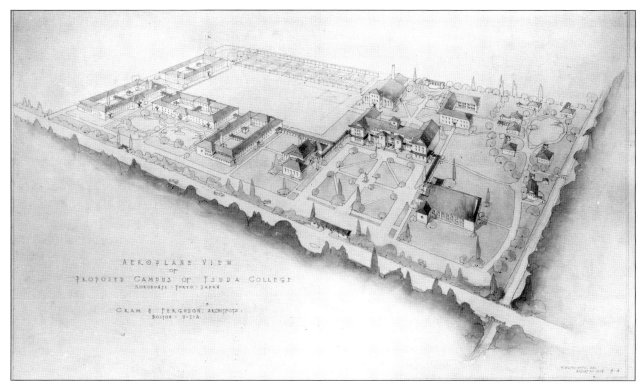

Perspective rendering of Tsuda campus plan.
(HDB/Cram & Ferguson Archive)

Rendering of Administration Building, artist
unknown. The design is different from Cram's previous work for an academic setting. The customary
classical or Gothic sculptural elements have been
replaced by geometric patterning like that of the de
Stijl movement. The transparent and reflective
qualities of glass highlight the interplay between
solid and void. (HDB/Cram & Ferguson Archive)

Rosary College (now Dominican University)
River Forest, Illinois, 1920

The original building group of the campus (then called Rosary College), the main quadrangle, was designed by Cram and Ferguson in a Gothic style sufficiently simple to provide an extendable template for later buildings. The result was a large, unified complex of low-rise buildings clustered around intimate courtyards.

Right: Doorway detail, 2006. (HDB/Cram & Ferguson Archive; photo: Ethan Anthony)

Below: The cloistered courtyard, based broadly on the architectural schema of Oxford University, included elements such as parapets, bays, and Gothic arches. (HDB/Cram & Ferguson Archive; photo: Ethan Anthony)

St. George's Chapel
Newport, Rhode Island, 1923–29

John Nicholas Brown's endowment of a new chapel for his alma mater, St. George's School, gave Cram the opportunity to demonstrate anew that the Gothic was a living style, adaptable for use in the twentieth century beyond mere copying. Brown was one of the wealthiest men in the country when his father and uncle died within weeks of each other in 1900. Still, the cost of the chapel, at nearly a million dollars, strained even the donor's budget though it was completed largely as planned.

St. George's Chapel complements the existing brick-and-stone Elizabethan classroom building, to which it is attached in part with a small polygonal turret, constructed with both the brick of the old building and the stone of the new chapel as a visual transition. The chapel is dramatically sited, overlooking two broad beaches.

Both the interior and exterior of the chapel are richly decorated with carving by John Evans. Crowning the stair turret is a ring of stone with gargoyles depicting several school officials, including the donor, John Nicholas Brown, and Cram and his partner Chester Brown.

Exterior. (HDB/Cram & Ferguson Archive; photo: Paul J. Weber)

Interior. The great west window was painted on clear glass to simulate stained glass as a cost-saving measure; it was so well done that it was never replaced even when funds were available. (HDB/Cram & Ferguson Archive; photo: P. E. Genereux)

Cloister showing the only fan vaulting Cram ever employed. This cloister was the first of four that were planned, and the only one that was completed. (HDB/Cram & Ferguson Archive; photo: Sigurd Fischer)

Detail of tower. Along the bell deck are the shields of many places of significance, including Connecticut, Jerusalem, Rome, and Canterbury. Exterior molding-stops include grotesques symbolizing events in the daily life of the St. George student such as student football and baseball and, in a nod to the origins of the fortune that financed the building, a variety of famous sailing ships. (HDB/Cram & Ferguson Archive; photo: Paul J. Weber)

The great stone boss at the height of the main vault depicts a brilliantly painted St. George slaying the dragon, shown here in the sculptor's submittal. (HDB/Cram & Ferguson Archive)

Choate School
Wallingford, Connecticut, 1924–25

Archbold Building (infirmary), 1925.

Cram's masterpiece, now renovated to serve as the administrative office of the school, possesses a distinctive and distinguished presence.

Left: Entry elevation. (HDB/Cram & Ferguson Archive; photo: E. W. Thompson)

Below left: Pond view. (HDB/Cram & Ferguson Archive; photo: E. W. Thompson)

Seymour St. John Chapel, 1924.

Top: Like Wheaton Chapel (see page 143), this design draws heavily from Christopher Wren churches. (HDB/Cram & Ferguson Archive)

Bottom: Interior. (HDB/Cram & Ferguson Archive)

University of Notre Dame
South Bend, Indiana, 1927

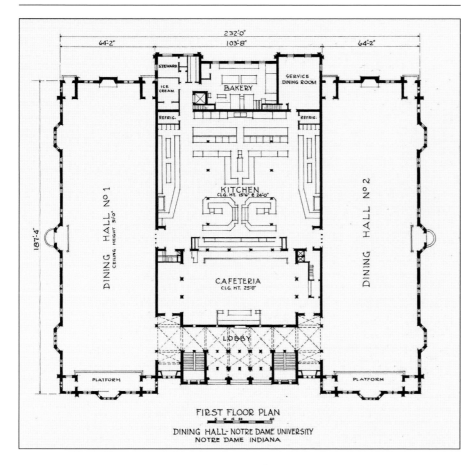

FIRST FLOOR PLAN

DINING HALL - NOTRE DAME UNIVERSITY
NOTRE DAME INDIANA

A tour-de-force of English neo-Gothic beam and stone, the dining hall at Notre Dame is an interesting addition to the remainder of the campus, a colder McGuiness-inspired Gothic Revival style. Cram's warmth and originality stand out in adding a lively presence and contrast to the gray stone that surrounds it.

Left: Plan. (HDB/Cram & Ferguson Archive)

Below: View from the quad. c. 1927. (HDB/Cram & Ferguson Archive; photo: Paul J. Weber)

Top: Entry elevation of dining hall.
(HDB/Cram & Ferguson Archive;
photo: Paul J. Weber)

Bottom: Groin-vaulted lobby arcade.
(HDB/Cram & Ferguson Archive)

Above: Interior of dining hall of Notre Dame. (HDB/Cram & Ferguson Archive)

Right: Interior view, c.1927. (HDB/Cram & Ferguson Archive; photo: Tebbs & Knell Inc.)

St. Paul's School
Concord, New Hampshire, 1927–37

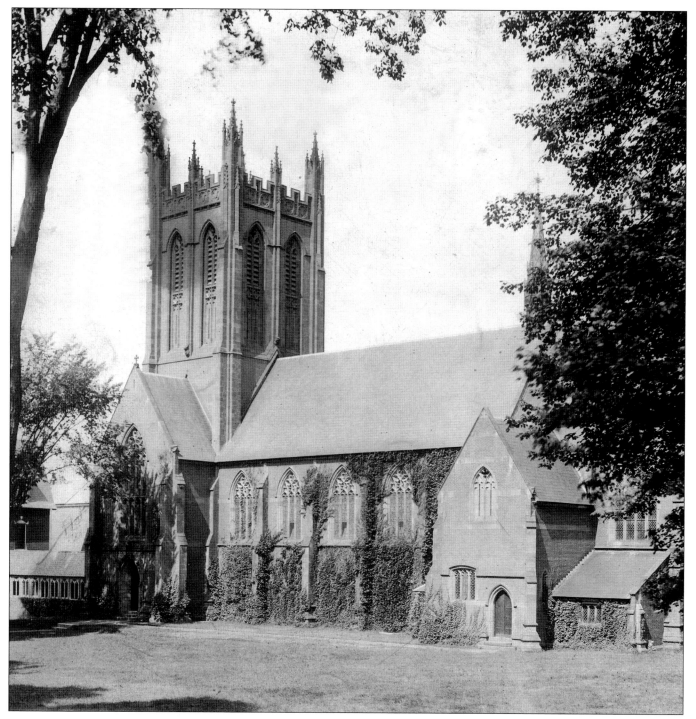

Henry Vaughan designed St. Paul's Chapel, the main
structure shown above. Cram added a new east end
(its entry shown at right), doubling the size of the
chapel. (HDB/Cram & Ferguson Archive)

St. Alban's Choir School
Washington, D.C., 1929

Renderings, artists unknown, for a proposed choir school at the National Cathedral.

Top: View of school showing fit of the building to the site. (HDB/Cram & Ferguson Archive; photo: R. M. Shaw)

Center: Side view. (HDB/Cram & Ferguson Archive; photo: William H. Pierce)

Bottom: Chapel view, alternate scheme. (HDB/Cram & Ferguson Archive)

Gibson Chapel, The Blue Ridge School
Dyke, Virginia, 1929

The Blue Ridge School was one of a number of schools founded by the Rt. Rev. Robert Atkinson Gibson, sixth Episcopal Bishop of Virginia, to bring education to impoverished children in the western Virginia Mountains. The school lacked the funds to pay an architect and Bishop Gibson, who had been rector at St. James in Richmond (Elizabeth Cram's family church), asked Cram to donate the design. Though various churches of Cram's country chapel type may have been modeled on the church at Llandudno in Wales, the massing, buttressing, and windows resemble the Abbot's Barn at Glastonbury Abbey, another site he visited.

Rendering of chapel. (HDB/Cram & Ferguson Archive; photo: R. M. Shaw)

Rollins College Chapel
Winter Park, Florida, 1930

Knowles Memorial Chapel is the last Spanish inspired church Cram designed. The tower is inspired by church towers in Segovia and Sevilla, the closest in proportion being that of famous Giralda in Sevilla. The Giralda or Weathervane was originally constructed as a mosque and then the upper stories were added in the 16th century after the Christian re-conquest of Spain. This combination of Muslim and Christian influences fascinated Cram because he believed many Christian forms had originated in Muslim lands.

Spanish Gothic pinnacles are combined with squared simplified buttresses for a "modern" result. (HDB/Cram & Ferguson Archive)

The Circular window in the west front and the decorated west door recall earlier churches such as the Cathedral at Dodge City and Holy Trinity in Havana designed with Goodhue. Rendering. (HDB/Cram & Ferguson Archive; photo: R. M. Shaw)

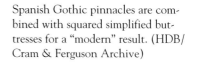

View of nave looking toward the altar. (HDB/Cram & Ferguson Archive)

University of Southern California
Los Angeles, California, 1930

Rendering of Doheny Library, designed with associate Sam Lunden and Frederick Law Olmsted's sons. The design is a blend of Norman, Hellenistic, and Justinian motifs with richly patterned brickwork modeled after medieval eastern Mediterranean precedents. The massing, central arch, windows, and masonry treatments follow the Byzantine model that Cram and his partners first used at Rice Institute. (HDB/Cram & Ferguson Archive; photo: Putnam)

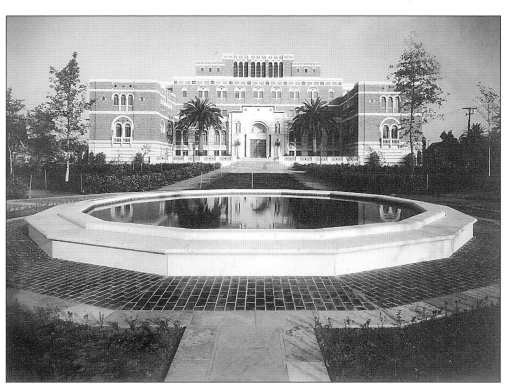

Alumni Plaza (HDB/Cram & Ferguson Archive; photo: Padilla Studios)

Doheny Library lobby. (HDB/ Cram & Ferguson Archive; photo: Padilla Studios)

A processional stairway leads from the entrance up to the reading hall. (HDB/Cram & Ferguson Archive; photo: Padilla Studios)

Wellesley College
Wellesley, Massachusetts, 1930

Top: The Student Alumni Building, part of a master plan by Cram, provides a large central meeting hall for the college. (HDB/Cram & Ferguson Archive; photo: Paul J. Weber)

Bottom: Side view. (HDB/Cram & Ferguson Archive; photo: Paul J. Weber)

Boston University
Boston, Massachusetts, 1930–66

Boston University might have been the great modernist Gothic project of Cram's career had the work been realized in full. Commissioned in 1930, Cram intended to incorporate a massive tower based on the Boston "Stump" as an entrance to a quiet green quadrangle. The scheme would have created an inner sanctum that juxtaposed the noisy city and the quiet precincts of academia inside. As with Sweet Briar, the scheme was so grand it was only partially realized; changing tastes brought a wave of extreme concrete buildings. Though the College of Liberal Arts, the College of Theology, and the chapel of the plan were completed, the master plan was abandoned in the 1960s.

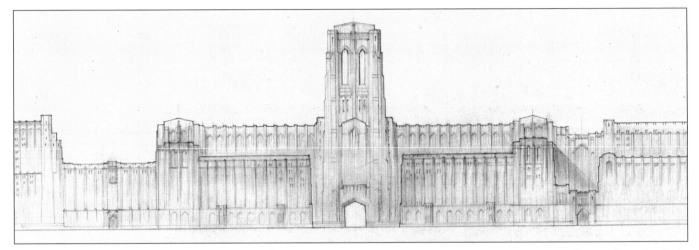

Frank Cleveland's masterful sketches portray an urban academic village ahead of its time and evocative of a powerful urban vision. The Liberal Arts and Theology Buildings (below) show the streamlined profiling associated with the 1930s, combined with touches of the English Perpendicular Gothic. The traditional chapel (not shown), completed by Hoyle and Doran after his death, was a Cram touch to emphasize the university's religious origins. (HDB/Cram & Ferguson Archive)

GROUP OF BUILDINGS FOR BOSTON UNIVERSITY

Model, 1930, showing Boston University master plan,
with a Tower of Learning modeled on the Boston "Stump"
and the chapel at the center of the scheme. (HDB/Cram
& Ferguson Archive; photo: Arthur C. Haskell)

St. Mary's High School and Grammar School
Glens Falls, New York, 1930

The building carries many of the themes from Frank Cleveland's
Boston University schemes to completion. A large institution fitted on
a tight city block, with Gothic details throughout, St. Mary's is a masterpiece of modern urban Gothic design.

Rendering, artist unknown. (HDB/
Cram & Ferguson Archive; photo:
R. M Shaw)

Swarthmore College
Swarthmore, Pennsylvania, 1938

Master plan for buildings not built because of the Depression and World War II.

Top: A clear change toward stripped classical style can be seen in the library design. (HDB/Cram & Ferguson Archive; photo: Rollin W. Bailey)

Bottom: Science building. (HDB/Cram & Ferguson Archive; photo: Rollin W. Bailey)

4. Residential, Institutional, and Commercial Architecture

The residential work of Ralph Adams Cram and his office demonstrates the progression from early to mature practice. The 1882 "cottage" sketches published in *Builder and Woodworker* are immature, but when Cram's work was realized, it soon displayed his self-assured and masterly management of massing. Cram admitted in his autobiography that the early work was conventional and of a sort then being done by many others, but his handling of Arts and Crafts detail distinguishes it from other work of the time. The proportions and organization of the houses improved continuously, and commissions increased in scope and budget. From 1900 on, the houses are larger and more elaborate: shingle, stucco, and half-timber are replaced by brick or stone, slate, and copper.

The sixteen examples of Cram's residential work contained in this section—from early work such as the Eddy house to the Brown, Atwood, and Taggert manor houses and summer "cottage"—illustrate a wide range of influences, from early English-inspired work to design drawn heavily from Cram's summers in France.

Cram's memorials are vestigial churches. The bell towers of Richmond, the chapel of Belleau Wood, the open-air chancel of Fère-en-Tardenois, and the chantry tomb of Woodrow Wilson each explore a portion of traditional ecclesiastical fabric expressed as a monumental statement.

Cram designed libraries throughout his career; several on collegiate and boarding school campuses are included in the Academic section of this book. The earliest public libraries, at Fall River (Massachusetts), Pawtucket (Rhode Island), and Nashua (New Hampshire), explored classical and Elizabethan themes and are represented here. Later academic and public libraries are Colonial or Georgian, save the Parker Hill Branch of the Boston Public Library, which reprises Gothic themes.

This section also illustrates some of the firm's office-building commissions. This building type did not play an important role in the firm's work until after Cram's death, when it became one of the most important forms for the office. The earliest office building, for the National Life Insurance Company in Montpelier, Vermont, was followed by a commission for New England Mutual Life Insurance Company (now New York Life). None of these projects held Cram's interest; they were largely the work of John T. Doran and Alexander Hoyle, both highly accomplished designers with their own followings. The McCormack Federal Building in Boston's Post Office Square did consume Cram's attention, though the commission was flawed by excessive government interference in the design process.

Finally, this section includes Cram's bridges over the Cape Cod Canal and his work rebuilding the historic waterfront of Portsmouth, New Hampshire.

Eddy Residence
Newton, Massachusetts, 1888

View from the street, 2005. The Eddy house bears a close resemblance to early unbuilt designs published in the periodical *Builder and Woodworker*. Here Cram first experimented with the oriel, indicating the stair, and the Palladian window. (HDB/Cram & Ferguson Archive; photo: Ethan Anthony)

Edward Courtland Gale Residence
Williamstown, Massachusetts, 1890

"Casa Lorna," Cram's house for Edward C. Gale, burned in the 1970s, when it was in service as a fraternity house at Williams College. (HDB/Cram & Ferguson Archive; photo: Richard Creek)

11 Kennedy Road
Cambridge, Massachusetts, c.1890

View from the street, 2005. The Cram-designed house has been altered almost beyond recognition: his signature dormers remain, but the original trim was stripped away during the 1970s. (HDB/Cram & Ferguson Archive; photo: Ethan Anthony)

Eugene Fellner Residence
Aspinwall Hill, Brookline, Massachusetts, 1890

Early in their partnership, Cram and Wentworth received commissions for the Fellner and Hamlin houses in a new subdivision named after its developer, Richard H. Aspinwall. Occupying a gentle hill in the streetcar suburb of Brookline, the site was planned by Frederick Law Olmsted, whose scheme for curving streets maintained the natural contours of the hill. The half-tim- bered Fellner house was modeled on Leyswood, Richard Norman Shaw's 1866 "old English" masterpiece of medieval English vernacular architecture. Publication of the Fellner house appears to have had a wide impact on American domestic architecture: Frank Lloyd Wright's Nathan Moore house employs aspects of its details

Rendering, artist unknown. (HDB/ Cram & Ferguson Archive, office reprint from *American Architect & Building News*, Mar. 11, 1893)

126 and 128 Brattle Street
Cambridge, Massachusetts, 1892

Two of three English Arts and Crafts–style houses in Cambridge demonstrating Cram's early interest in the style. The photographs, taken in 2005, show the houses largely as-built, though interiors have been altered by modern architects.

128 Brattle Street, view from street. (HDB/Cram & Ferguson Archive; photo: Ethan Anthony)

126 Brattle Street. (HDB/Cram & Ferguson Archive; photo: Ethan Anthony)

165 Winthrop Street
Aspinwall Hill, Brookline, Massachusetts, c.1892

This house, photographed in 2005, is attributed to Cram, but it is not known for whom it was originally designed. It may be the house for Mr. Hamlin or the Hamlin family. (HDB/Cram & Ferguson Archive; photo: Ethan Anthony)

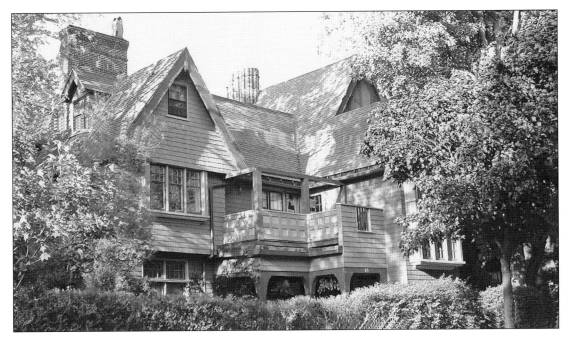

Bushy Hill
Simsbury, Connecticut, 1893

Bushy Hill, a residence designed for Walter Phelps Dodge Esq., represents Cram's mature Arts and Crafts design. (HDB/Cram & Ferguson Archive, office reprint from *American Architect & Building News*, Mar. 27, 1893)

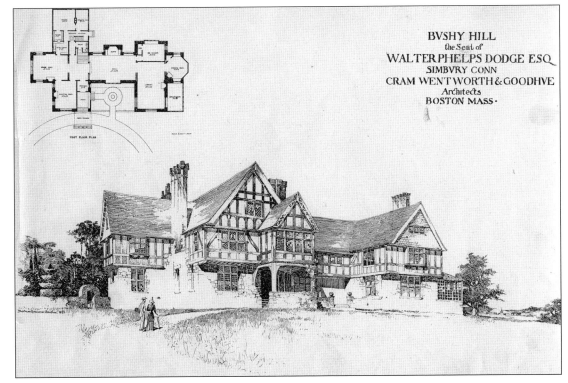

Richmond Court Apartments
Brookline, Massachusetts, 1898

Richmond Court represented a move in a new direction— Elizabethan—perhaps in part a response to its easy adaptability to Boston's familiar red brick. Here it is combined with limestone lintels and trim. Limestone was easier to work than the local Quincy granite and provided new color combinations Cram preferred over the heaviness of brownstone. Cram was moving from Richardson's French and German precedents to an English model he promoted as more appropriate for the predominantly English immigrants that were his clients.

Left and opposite page: Goodhue's renderings echo the distinctive stonework of Hampton Court Palace in England. (HDB/Cram & Ferguson Archive, office reprint from *American Architect & Building News,* Mar. 27, 1893)

Rederings of the entry courtyard from Beacon Street (top) and the first floor overlooking a fountain. (HDB/Cram & Ferguson Archive, office reprint from *America Architect & Building News*, Mar. 18, 1899)

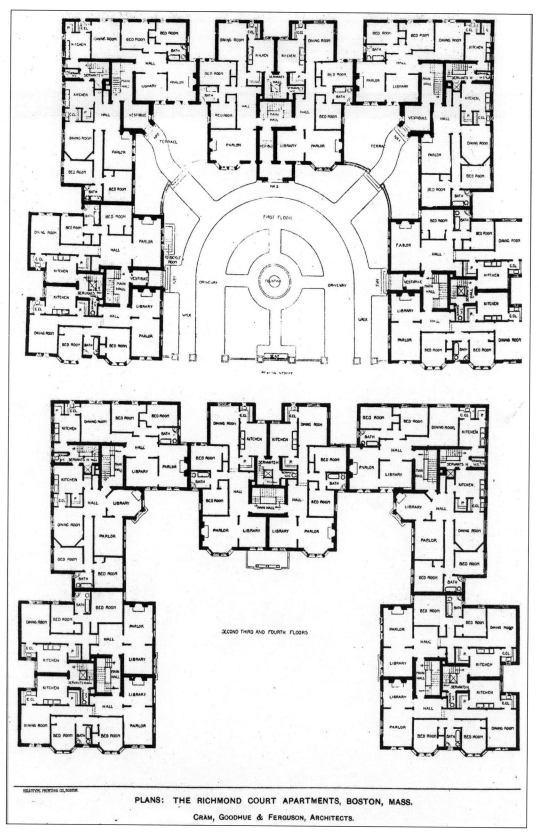

PLANS: THE RICHMOND COURT APARTMENTS, BOSTON, MASS.

CRAM, GOODHUE & FERGUSON, ARCHITECTS.

Plans of Richmond Court. (HDB/Cram & Ferguson Archive, office reprint from *America Architect & Building News*, Mar. 18, 1899)

Harbor Court
Newport, Rhode Island, 1904

John Nicholas Brown, heir to a great family mercantile fortune, assisted Cram in his effort to encourage patronage of the arts. Brown served as treasurer for the Medieval Academy of America, which he and Cram founded together with several Harvard professors. After Brown's death, his wife gave Cram and Goodhue their largest residential commission to date, the Browns' summer cottage, another echo of Cram's travels in France.

Entry facade. (HDB/Cram & Ferguson Archive; photo: Thomas Ellison)

Charles Barron Residence
Beacon Street, Boston, Massachusetts, 1907

The Charles Barron residence is the first example of Cram's growing interest in medieval French vernacular. (He and his family rented a house outside Paris, where he spent several summers exploring and photographing.) The house is predominant-ly stucco, as were the Brittany chateaus on which it was based, an unexpected material for Boston's mostly brick Back Bay. The design includes doorframes of carved granite and dormers and oriels clad in copper.

The view from Beacon Street. (HDB/Cram & Ferguson Archive; photo: Ethan Anthony)

Front door. (HDB/Cram & Ferguson Archive; photo: Ethan Anthony)

House on the Moors
Gloucester, Massachusetts, 1917

The town of Gloucester, with its fishing boats and granite out-crops, was attractive to artists, who worked by day and attended glittering parties and art exhibitions at night. William and Emmeline Abbot Atwood were two painters who summered there and commissioned Cram to build a summer "cottage." Their House on the Moors is in the form of a medieval gatehouse majestically sited atop a stone arch that bridges two outcrops of pink granite. The first residence Cram designed after Goodhue's departure from the partnership, it is a powerful reprise of Arts-and-Crafts themes they had explored earlier. Simple half-timbered dormers punctuate long, unbroken ridgelines. The large stones of the arch seem an extension of the granite underneath. A five-acre park with a pond and rowboats was available for visitors who came to paint and play.

Entrance facade. (HDB/Cram & Ferguson Archive)

House on the Moors.

Top: Approach to the gallery under the house. (HDB/Cram & Ferguson Archive)

Bottom: Half-timber gable front. (HDB/Cram & Ferguson Archive)

The interiors of the House on the Moors are clad in warm-toned wood under a beamed ceiling and fitted with Arts and Crafts wrought-iron fittings.

Top to bottom: Tile, wrought iron, and heavy woodwork in the living room; the morning room, and the art gallery. (HDB/Cram & Ferguson Archive)

Blanche Sewall Residence
Houston, Texas, 1924

For Blanche Sewall's house in the Houston suburbs, Cram was able to apply the Mexican and Mediterranean themes with which Goodhue had experimented.

Entry facade. (HDB/Cram & Ferguson Archive; photo: Mike Ortega, 2006)

Garden view. (HDB/Cram & Ferguson Archive; photo: Mike Ortega, 2006)

Front door of the Sewall residence. (HDB/Cram & Ferguson Archive)

Entry drive. (HDB/Cram & Ferguson Archive; photo: Mike Ortega, 2006)

Paul Watkins House
Winona, Minnesota, 1925

An extraordinary French Gothic manor house similar to Harbor Court (see page 209), the Watkins house is constructed of elegantly proportioned patterned brick.

Facade. (HDB/Cram & Ferguson Archive)

Detail of porch. (HDB/ Cram & Ferguson Archive)

Angelica Livingston Gerry Residence
Lake Delaware, New York, 1926

This was a house of reinforced concrete (unusual for a residence) for Angelica Gerry, heiress to a Manhattan real estate fortune. Within the neo-Georgian skin resided an asymmetrical plan. Gerry had commissioned Cram to design St. James Church at Lake Delaware. She named the house AnCram, a conjunction of their names.

The house was demolished in the 1970s as a result of a tax dispute with the town.

Above: Rendering, artist unknown, 1925. (HDB/Cram & Ferguson Archive)

Right: Photograph from Angelica Gerry's construction scrapbook of the AnCram home. (HDB/Cram & Ferguson Archive)

Chickamauga Memorial Arch
Chickamauga, Tennessee, 1897

Rendering of an early project for a commemorative arch at the Confederate battleground in Tennessee. (HDB/Cram & Ferguson Archive; photo: Richard Creek)

Washington Hotel
Colón, Panama, 1910

Commissioned by President Taft, the office designed the hotel for the Panama Railroad Company. The hotel was a melding of churrigueresque and Mexican themes. (From Ralph Emmett Avery, *America's Triumph in Panama*, Chicago: L. W. Walter Co., 1913)

Edward Courtland Gale Mausoleum
Troy, New York, 1914

Though it was said of Cram that he built his own monuments, he also built the monuments of his friends. The largest of Cram's many private memorials, the Gale Mausoleum is a simple Gothic memorial for a lifelong friend and client, a successful department store owner and trustee of Williams College. Bearing walls of solid granite blocks support a reinforced concrete roof slab. Four functional buttresses frame the carved limestone surround over the bronze door.

Buttresses and an elaborate Gothic Perpendicular door decorate a simple volume in granite. (HDB/Cram & Ferguson Archive; photo: Ethan Anthony)

Woodrow Wilson Memorial
Washington DC, 1925

Cram's monument for Woodrow Wilson, a central figure in Cram's career, is in Washington National Cathedral. It resembles the biers of knights that Cram saw in many Gothic churches and cathedrals across Europe. (HDB/Cram & Ferguson Archive)

Memorial Chapel, American Military Cemetery
Belleau Wood, France, 1926

One of two World War I memorials Cram was commissioned to design, Belleau Wood was the site of a ferocious battle where more than five thousand American Marines died. Cram created a neo-Norman tower housing a chapel where the names of the dead are engraved on the walls.

Right: View of the memorial chapel under construction. (HDB/Cram & Ferguson Archive)

Below: the entrance gate. (HDB/Cram & Ferguson Archive)

Columbus Memorial Competition
Santo Domingo, Dominican Republic, 1929

Design for an international competition to commemorate the discovery of the New World held by the Organization of American States. The jury included Raymond Hood and Eliel Saarinen; the Cram entry was awarded an honorable mention.

Right: Rendering of competition, elevation, artist unknown. (HDB/Cram & Ferguson Archive; photo: Paul J. Weber)

Below: General view of competition design.(HDB/Cram & Ferguson Archive; photo: Paul J. Weber)

THE CHRISTOPHER COLUMBUS
MEMORIAL LIGHTHOUSE COMPETITION

World War I Memorial Carillon
Richmond, Virginia, 1926

Despite Cram's extensive association with Virginia through his marriage and his work at Sweet Briar College and the University of Richmond, the selection of a Boston firm to design an important state monument was controversial, so Cram appointed as associate architect the Richmond native Marcellus Wright, a finalist in the competition and local architect for much of Cram's work for the University of Richmond.

Cram proposed a tower housing a carillon—a classical Christopher Wren steeple set upon a plain brick shaft.

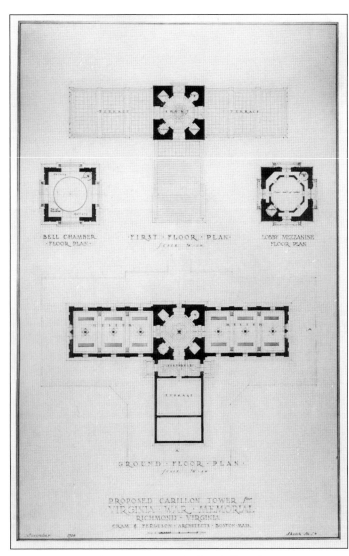

Plan. The ground floor is a memorial gallery still used for exhibitions. (HDB/Cram & Ferguson Archive)

Rendering of the carillon by R. K. Fletcher, 1926. (HDB/Cram & Ferguson Archive)

View of the memorial, 1992. (HDB/Cram &
Ferguson Archive; photo: Ethan Anthony)

Oise-Aisne American Military Cemetery Memorial
Fère-en-Tardenois, France, 1926

At the site of a World War I military cemetery, Cram framed the surrounding French landscape with a colonnade of fine marble columns capped with carved Norman capitals supporting Romanesque arches. The composition is Cram's most abstract and one of his most modern in concept. A chancel surrounds a symbolic altar open to the sky; the ambulatory colonnade separates the place of the battle from the symbolic altar of sacrifice. Vestigial "towers" frame the entry to the chancel and the raised predella. Paul Cret was the consulting architect for the American Military Cemetery Commission.

View from memorial. (HDB/Cram & Ferguson Archive; photo: Cherojon)

View from cemetery. (HDB/Cram & Ferguson Archive; photo: Cherojon)

Deborah Cook Sayles Public Library
Pawtucket, Rhode Island, 1893

Entrance facade, 1902. The plan is symmetrical, with the circulation desk at the center flanked by a reading room and the stacks. Here Cram and Goodhue looked to the English classical revival and specifically at the precedent of Robert Adam's Kedleston Hall. (HDB/Cram & Ferguson Archive)

Plan. (HDB/Cram & Ferguson Archive)

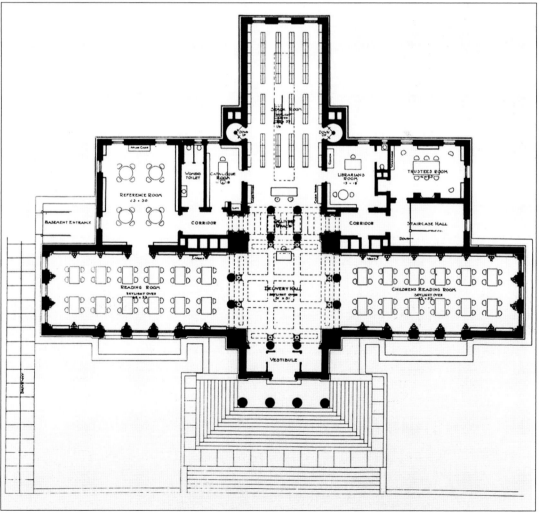

Public Library
Fall River, Massachusetts, 1899

Cram and Goodhue designed three public libraries in their years together—the Sayles Library, shown on previous page, the library in Fall River (left), and the Hunt Library in Nashua (below). The parti in Fall River is a small Palladian pavilion with its center temple front thrust forward, shown here in a rendering, artist unknown. (HDB/Cram & Ferguson Archive; photo: Richard Creek)

Hunt Library
Nashua, New Hampshire, 1902

Cram and Goodhue chose to discard the classical motifs attempted in their earlier libraries for a further experiment with Elizabethan themes. A powerful tower drawn from Oxford models replaces the Soane-like dome planned for Fall River. It marks the circulation desk and brings light down into the center of the building. Glass floors, strategically placed, beautify the circulation with filtered natural light. Elaborate carvings decorate the coping over the facade that faces downtown, and large limestone blocks on the main street elevation, presumably intended for the eventual carving of the likenesses of the donors. (HDB/Cram & Ferguson Archive; photo: Clark)

The interior of Hunt Library features an adult and a children's reading room lined with fumed oak shelving and a grand public hearth decorated with Mercer tiles and a Latin inscription.

Top: Reading room. (HDB/Cram & Ferguson Archive; photo: Clark)

Bottom: Detail of fireplace. (HDB/Cram & Ferguson Archive, photo: Clark)

Lucius Beebe Memorial Library
Wakefield, Massachusetts, 1921

The elegant English Renaissance/Palladian Beebe foreshadows two similar classical designs for college libraries at Wheaton and Sweet Briar (see pages 142 and 146). The elaborate interior was based on measured drawings of English precedents. (HDB/Cram & Ferguson Archive; photo: Paul J. Weber)

Houston Public Library
Houston, Texas, 1926

The Houston Public Library, designed in collaboration with William Ward Watkin, who ran Cram's Houston office. The front is unsymmetricalt; the main building and the garden are strangely off-center and a wing seems to have been added after the fact. The stone-clad walls are punctuated with large Romanesque windows and capped, uncharacteristically for Cram, by low Mediterranean rooflines. (HDB/Cram & Ferguson Archive; photo: Paul J. Weber)

Facade of the Houston Public Library, with Spanish details added in a mannerist fashion to a Romanesque building. (HDB/Cram & Ferguson Archive)

Plan. Watkin's strength was in interior design, and here the Houston Library does not disappoint: its interior is organized around a dramatic multistory central hall that connects the wings on each level and is a successful organizer for the building. (HDB/Cram & Ferguson Archive)

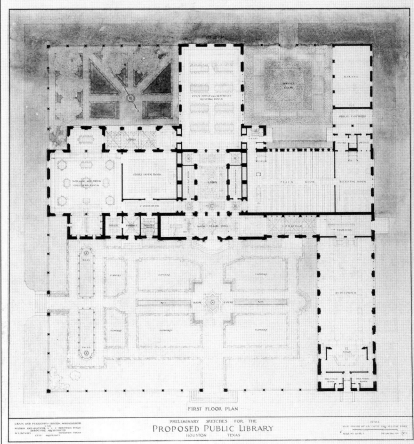

Parker Hill Branch, Boston Public Library
Roxbury, Massachusetts, 1929

BRANCH·LIBRARY·BUILDING·
·IN·PARKER·HILL·DISTRICT·
THE·CITY·OF·BOSTON·

CRAM·AND·FERGUSON·ARCHITECTS·
·BOSTON·   ·MASSACHUSETTS·

Rendering, artist unknown, of the Parker Hill Branch Library, one of two branches the firm designed for the Boston Public Library system. The Parker Hill branch is clad in granite with fine Gothic windows. In spite of its rather modest size it has a powerful presence. (HDB/Cram & Ferguson Archive; photo: R. M. Shaw)

New York City Hall Competition
New York, New York, 1893

Perspective drawing, artist unknown, of an unsuccessful competition entry for a proposed City Hall. (HDB/ Cram & Ferguson Archive)

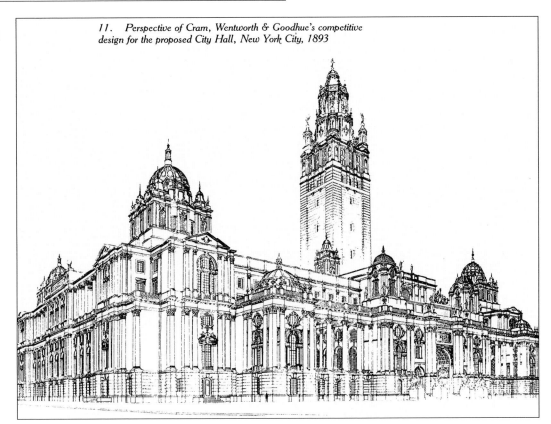

11.   Perspective of Cram, Wentworth & Goodhue's competitive design for the proposed City Hall, New York City, 1893

Diet Building
Tokyo, Japan, 1899

Rendering by Goodhue of proposal for a new Japanese parliament building, not built. (HDB/ Cram & Ferguson Archive)

National Life Insurance Building
Montpelier, Vermont, 1921

OFFICE BUILDING FOR
NATIONAL LIFE INSURANCE COMPANY
MONTPELIER VERMONT
CRAM AND FERGUSON ARCHITECTS BOSTON MASS.

Rendering, possibly by Frank Cleveland, for a Colonial-style office building, the commission that launched Cram's firm as the preeminent designers of insurance company headquarters for the first half of the twentieth century. (HDB/Cram & Ferguson Archive)

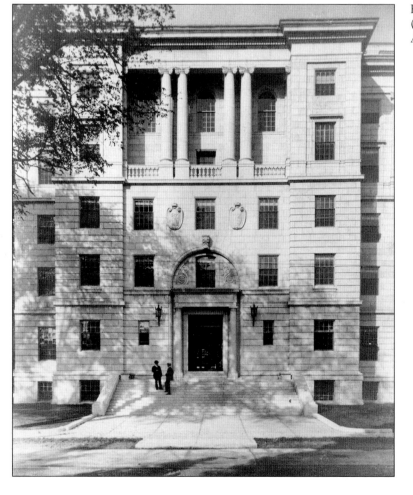

Early photograph of the entry. (HDB/Cram & Ferguson Archive)

McCormack Federal Building
Boston, Massachusetts, 1929

With its streamlined Art Deco profile, the McCormack Building was the closest the firm came to building a "modern" skyscraper. Cram was profoundly disappointed when the General Services Administration did not allow him to design the mass of the building, but limited him to decorating the surface.

Rendering, possibly by John Doran. (HDB/Cram & Ferguson Archive; photo: R. M. Shaw)

Elevation. (HDB/Cram & Ferguson Archive; photo: R. M. Shaw)

Portsmouth Harbor Front Renewal
Portsmouth, New Hampshire, 1933

The Prescott sisters, lifelong Portsmouth residents and heirs of their brother's fortune, commissioned Cram, a distant cousin, to redesign the waterfront area of the city where they had spent their childhood above their father's butcher shop. Their objective was to demolish the entire declining warehouse area and replace it with an environment that harkened back to an earlier time.

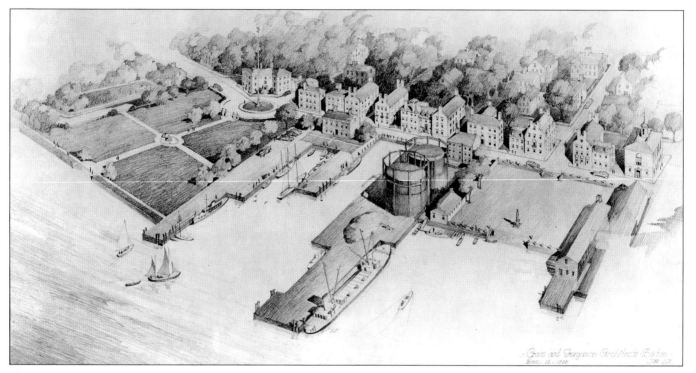

Above: Rendering, artist unknown. (HDB/Cram & Ferguson Archive)

Below left: View of the broad avenue leading to the park before Cram's design. (HDB/Cram & Ferguson Archive)

Below right: After photograph of the area lined with relocated and restored historic houses. (HDB/Cram & Ferguson Archive)

District Court Building
Dedham, Massachusetts, 1937

Cram designed several courthouses and public and corporate buildings using the classical imperial Roman temple theme.

Top: Rendering, artist unknown. (HDB/Cram & Ferguson Archive; photo: Arthur C. Haskell)

Bottom: Entry facade. (HDB/Cram & Ferguson Archive)

PROPOSED DISTRICT COURT BUILDING · · DEDHAM · MASSACHUSETTS ·

Holy Cross Monastery
West Park, New York, 1934

Bell tower and chapel for the monastery of the Episcopal Brotherhood of the Society of St. John the Evangelist on the Hudson River, not far from West Point. The tower here is simple. (HDB/Cram & Ferguson Archive, office reprint from unknown source; photo: Paul J. Weber)

HOLY CROSS MONASTERY, WEST PARK, NEW YORK—VIEW FROM THE SOUTHWEST

Bourne and Sagamore Bridges
Cape Cod, Massachusetts, 1938

These two bridges were unusual projects for the Cram firm.

Top: The massive concrete pylons of the Bourne Bridge are a distinctive gateway to Cape Cod Canal. (HDB/Cram & Ferguson Archive; photo: Arthur C. Haskell)

Bottom: Cram won the award for the most beautiful bridge of 1938 for the Sagamore Bridge, which uses Romanesque and Gothic arch and tower forms as inspiration. (HDB/Cram & Ferguson Archive; photo: Arthur C. Haskell)

New England Mutual Life Insurance Headquarters
Boston, Massachusetts, 1938

Cram and Ferguson's transition from eclecticism to the International Style of the 1950s can be seen in the stripped classical styling of this building. Despite the increasing severity of its massing, there is still a wealth of detail. Carved granite reliefs and column capitals, bronze doors and screens, and atop it all four granite funerary urns complete a typical Cram "joke." In fact, Cram did not approve of the design shown in this rendering, largely the work of his partners. Soon after Cram's death, New England Life commissioned the firm to design a massive addition that filled the block and resulted in a more satisfying urban solution.

Rendering. (HDB/Cram & Ferguson Archive)

The People's Savings Bank
Providence, Rhode Island, 1944

Two years after Cram's death the transition begun with the McCormack
Federal Building was complete. The classically composed but expressive
Art Deco People's Savings Bank shows the new direction of the firm.

Rendering by John T. Doran.
(HDB/Cram & Ferguson
Archive; photo: Sigurd
Fischer)

The John Hancock Life Insurance Company Headquarters Building

Boston, Massachusetts, 1946

The Hancock Building, now a fixture of the Boston skyline, mixes Art Deco with Mont-Saint-Michel, a fitting tribute in which Cram's partners bid adieu to the crusading knight.

Rendering by John T. Doran. (HDB/Cram & Ferguson Archive)

Project List

1882

Proposed Early Cottages, Boston, MA; (job #400); Residence

1883

John Sheppard, Lenox, MA; (job #401); Residence; Status unknown

1886

James M. Ide, Williamstown, MA; (job #402); Residence; Extant

1889

Eddy Residence, Newton Corner, MA; (job #63); Residence; Extant **(M)**

Knapp House, New Bedford, MA; (job #430); Residence; Extant

First Baptist Church, Brattleboro, VT; (job #446); Ecclesiastical

1890

Whitemore Residence, York Harbor, ME; (job #44); Burned

Stark House (job #403); Residence; Extant

Seaside Club House, Bridgeport, CT; (job #429); Residence; Extant

Eugene Faulkner Residence, Brookline, MA; (job #404); Residence; Extant

Fellner House, Brookline, MA; (job #407); Residence; Not extant **(M)**

E. C. Gale, "Casa Loma," Williamstown, MA; (job #409); Residence; Demolished **(M)**

1891

All Saints Church, Ashmont, MA; (job #47); Ecclesiastical; Extant **(I, R)**

St. Paul's Episcopal Church, Brockton, MA; (job #54); Ecclesiastical; Extant **(I, R)**

1892

128 Brattle Street, Cambridge, MA; (job #406); Residence; Extant **(M)**

126 Brattle Street, Cambridge, MA; Residence; Extant **(M)**

1893

Emmanuel Church, Wakefield, MA; (job #46); Ecclesiastical; Not extant

Deborah Cook Sayles Public Library, Pawtucket, RI; (job #48); Municipal; Extant

Walter Phelps Dodge, Simsbury, CT; (job #408); Residence; Not built **(M)**

Christ Church, Hyde Park, MA; Ecclesiastical; Extant **(R)**

Swedenborgian Church, Newtonville, MA; (job #964); Ecclesiastical; Extant (R)

Church of Saints Peter and Paul, Fall River, MA; (job #467); Ecclesiastical; Not Extant **(R)**

New York City Hall Competition, New York, NY; Government; Unsuccessful **(R)**

1894

First Congregational Church, Plymouth, MA; Status unknown

St. Andrew's, Detroit, MI

1895

Joseph Merrill, Little Boars Head, NH; (job #410); Residence; Status unknown

St. Luke's Church, Roxbury, MA; (job #458); Ecclesiastical; Extant **(R)**

All Saints Episcopal Church, Brookline, MA; Ecclesiastical **(I)**

Second Congregational Church, Exeter, NH; (job #457); Ecclesiastical; Extant **(I, R)**

1896

Christ Church, Waltham, MA

St. Paul's Church, Rochester, NY; Status unknown

1897

Chickamauga Arch, Chickamauga, TN; Memorial; Extant **(I, M)**

1898

Smith College, Northampton, MA; Master Plan

Church of our Saviour, Middleboro, MA; Status unknown

First Parrish Meeting House, Cambridge, MA

Richmond Court Apartments, Brookline, MA; (job # 434); Residence; Extant **(I, M)**

1899

Diet Building, Tokyo, Japan; Government; Not built **(M)**

Fall River Public Library, Fall River, MA; (job #443); Library; Extant **(M)**

St. Stephen's Episcopal Church, Cohasset, MA; Ecclesiastical; Extant **(R)**

1900

St. Stephen's Episcopal Church, Fall River, MA; (job #49); Ecclesiastical; Burned

11 Kennedy Road, Newton, MA; (job #411); Residence; Extant **(M)**

First Church, Cambridge, MA; alterations; Not built

Wheaton College, Norton, MA; Master Plan

Emmanuel Episcopal Church, Newport, RI; (job #621); Ecclesiastical; Extant **(R)**

1902

Groton School Seal, Groton, CT; (job #50); School seal

Strudwick House (Tamarind), Hillsborough, NC; (job #453); Residence attributed to Cram

St. Paul's Episcopal Church, Chicago, IL; (job #741); Furnishings; Hunt Memorial Library, Nashua, NH; Library; Extant **(M)**

1902

First Baptist Church, Pittsburgh, PA; (job #51); Ecclesiastical; Status unknown **(R)**

Sweet Briar College, Sweet Briar, VA; (job #607); Academic; Master Plan **(A)**

Sweet Briar College, Sweet Briar, VA; (job #612); Academic; Extant

Sweet Briar College, Sweet Briar, VA; (job #613); Academic; Extant

Sweet Briar College, Sweet Briar, VA; (job #614); Academic; Extant

Sweet Briar College, Sweet Briar, VA; (job #615); Academic; Rendering **(A)**

1903

St. John's Cathedral in the Wilderness, Denver, CO; (job #465); Ecclesiastical; Unsuccessful **(R)**

All Saints Chapel for University of the South, Sewanee, TN; (job #763); Academic; Extant **(R, A)**

Christ Church Cathedral, Victoria, British Columbia; (job #951); Ecclesiastical; Extant **(R)**

1904

U.S. Military Academy, West Point, NY; (job #104); School Chapel; Extant **(I, A)**

Proposed for E. H. Harriman, Arden, NY; (job #412); Residence; Not built

John Nicholas Brown-Harbor Court, Newport, RI; (job #414); Residence **(M)**

U.S. Military Army Academy, West Point, NY; (job #435); Officers Apartments; Extant

U.S. Military Academy, West Point, NY; Master Plan **(A)**

U.S. Military Academy, West Point, NY **(A)**

1905

St. John & St. James Church, Roxbury, MA; Ecclesiastical

First Unitarian Church, West Newton, MA; (job #691); Ecclesiastical; Extant **(R)**

1906

Los Angeles Cathedral, Los Angeles, CA; Ecclesiastical; Not built **(R)**

Glens Falls Presbyterian Church, Glens Falls, NY; (job #112); Ecclesiastical; Extant **(R)**

All Saints Cathedral, Halifax, Nova Scotia; (job #456); Ecclesiastical; Extant **(R)**

Westminster Presbyterian Church, Springfield, IL; Ecclesiastical; Extant **(R)**

Calvary Episcopal Church, Pittsburgh, PA; (job #817); Ecclesiastical; Extant **(I, R)**

1907

St. John's Church, Hartford, CT

Hoosac School, Hoosac, NY; (job #40); Academic; Status unknown

Rutgers University, New Brunswick, NJ; (job #42); Academic; Burned

St. Thomas Episcopal Church, New York City, NY; (job #52); Ecclesiastical; Extant **(I, R)**

Princeton University, Princeton, NJ; (job #53); Academic; Master Plan **(A)**

Charles W. Barron, Boston, MA; (job #436); Residence; Extant **(M)**

Trinity Memorial Church (Now St. Andrews), Denver, CO; (job #474); Ecclesiastical; Extant **(R)**

Church of the Covenant, Cleveland, OH; (job #571); Ecclesiastical; Unknown **(R)**

Christ Church Cathedral Plate, Hartford, CT; (job #632); Altar Cross / interiors; Ecclesiastical; Status unknown

St. Peter's & St. John Episcopal, Auburn, NY; (job #636); Ecclesiastical

1908

Christ Church, West Haven, CT

Russell Sage Memorial First, Far Rockaway, NY; Ecclesiastical, Extant **(R)**

St. Paul's Episcopal Cathedral, Detroit, MI; (job #109); Ecclesiastical; Extant **(R)**

St. Mary's Church, Walkerville, Ontario; (job #454); Ecclesiastical; Extant **(R)**

St. John's Parish, West Hartford, CT; (job #469); Ecclesiastical; Extant

Santissima Trinidad Cathedral, El Vedado, Havana, Cuba; (job#471); Ecclesiastical; Extant **(R)**

Cathedral of the Incarnation, Baltimore, MD; (job #473); Ecclesiastical; Not built **(R)**

Princeton University, Princeton, NJ: (job #657); Academic; Graduate College MP; Extant **(A)**

Proposed Church & Rectory, Guantanamo, Cuba; Ecclesiastical; Not Built

1909

St. Mark's, Mt. Kisco, NY

St. Helena's Episcopal Church, Boerne, TX; (job #55); Ecclesiastical; Not built

Rice University, Houston, TX; (job #56); Academic; Master Plan **(A)**

Princeton University, Princeton, NJ: (job #911); Academic; Extant **(A)**

1910

Lady Chapel for St. Paul's Church, New Haven, CT; Ecclesiastical; Extant

St. Mark's Episcopal Church, Mt. Kisco, NY; Ecclesiastical; Extant

Grace Church, Providence, RI; (job #57); Ecclesiastical; Extant

The Washington Hotel, Colon, Panama; (job #59); Hospitality; Extant **(M)**

University of Richmond, Richmond, VA; (job #100); Academic; Master Plan **(A)**

St. James Episcopal Church, West Hartford, CT; (job #124); Ecclesiastical; Status unknown

Ascension Episcopal Church, Montgomery, AL; (job #622); Ecclesiastical; Extant **(R)**

1911

St. Michael's Church Parish House, Milton, MA; Ecclesiastical; Extant

St. Mary's School, Peekskill, NY; (job #103); Academic; Extant **(A)**

Cathedral of St. John the Divine, New York City, NY; (job #501); Ecclesiastical; Extant

St. Paul's Episcopal Church, Malden, MA; (job #573); Ecclesiastical **(R)**

Sweet Briar College, Sweet Briar, VA; (job #608); Academic; Extant

Cathedral of St. John the Divine, New York City, NY; (job #630); Ecclesiastical; Extant

Grace Episcopal Church, Manchester, NH; (job #644A); Ecclesiastical; Status unknown **(R)**

St. James Episcopal Church, New York City, NY; (job #671); Ecclesiastical; Extant **(R)**

Phillips Exeter Academy, Exeter, NH; (job #678); Academic; Extant

Wheaton College, Norton, MA; (job #707); Academic; Extant

All Souls United Church of Christ, Bangor, ME; (job #803); Ecclesiastical; Status unknown

U.S. Military Academy, West Point, NY

1912

Rice University, Houston, TX; Academic; Extant **(A)**

Rice University, Houston, TX; Academic; Extant **(A)**

First Presbyterian Church, Oakland, CA; Ecclesiastical; Extant **(R)**

St. John and St. James Church, New Haven, CT; (job #58); Ecclesiastical; Extant

Williams College, Williamstown, MA; (job #64); Academic; Extant **(A)**

University of Richmond, Richmond, VA; (job #65); Academic; Extant **(A)**

University of Richmond, Richmond, VA; (job #66); Academic; Extant

University of Richmond, Richmond, VA; (job #67); Academic; Extant

Fourth Presbyterian Church, Chicago, IL; (job #107); Ecclesiastical; Extant **(R)**

Gate of Heaven Church, South Boston, MA; (job #131); Ecclesiastical, Extant

All Souls United Church of Christ, Bangor, ME; (job #139); Ecclesiastical; Status unknown

Church of the Savior, Syracuse, NY; (job #449), Ecclesiastical; Extant

RSGC (Cathedral of St. Alban the Martyr), Toronto, Ontario, Canada; (job #455); Ecclesiastical; Not Extant

Church of the New Jerusalem, Bryn Athyn, PA; (job #459); Ecclesiastical; Extant **(R)**

Christ Church, Hyde Park, MA; (job #669); Ecclesiastical; Extant

House of Hope Presbyterian Church, St. Paul, MN; (job #684); Ecclesiastical; Extant **(R)**

Wheaton College, Norton, MA; (job #672); Academic; Extant

Sweet Briar College, Sweet Briar, VA; (job #609); Academic; Extant

All Saints' Church Ashmont, Dorchester. MA; (job #723); Ecclesiastical, Extant

1913

Princeton University, Princeton, NJ; (job #72); Academic; Extant **(I)**

Whitehall, Sudbury, MA; (job #424); Residence; Extant

Grace Episcopal Church, Manchester, NH; (job #644); Ecclesiastical; Extant

All Saints Episcopal Church, Peterborough, NH; (job # 690); Ecclesiastical; Extant **(R)**

University of Richmond, Richmond, VA; (job #68); Academic; Extant

University of Richmond, Richmond, VA; (job #69); Academic; Extant

1914

Rice University, Houston, TX; Academic; Extant **(A)**

Edward Courtland Gale Mausoleum, Troy, NY; (job #60); Mausoleum; Extant **(M)**

St. John the Evangelist Episcopal, Newport, RI; (job #136); Ecclesiastical; Extant

Trinity Episcopal Church, Princeton, NJ; (job #561); Ecclesiastical; Extant (R)

St. Paul's Cathedral, Boston, MA; (job #619); Ecclesiastical; Demolished

Phillips Exeter Academy, Exeter, NH; (job #675); Academic; Status unknown (A)

St. Elizabeth Chapel, Sudbury, MA; (job #696); Ecclesiastical; Extant (R)

Chapel for the Sisters of St. Anne, Arlington Heights, MA; (job #710); Ecclesiastical; Extant (R)

St. Ignatius Episcopal Church, New York City, NY; (job #711); Ecclesiastical; Extant

1915

Wheaton College, Norton, MA; (job #662); Ecclesiastical; Extant (A)

1916

Sacred Heart Cathedral, Dodge City, KS; (job #41); Ecclesiastical; Extant (R)

First Universalist Church, Somerville, MA; (job #466); Ecclesiastical; Extant (R)

Mercersburg Academy Chapel, Mercersburg, PA; (job #592); School Chapel; Extant (A)

St. James Church, Richmond, VA; (job #682); Ecclesiastical; Burned

Wheaton College, Norton, MA; (job #706); Academic; Extant (A)

1917

House on the Moors, Gloucester, MA; Residential; Extant (M)

Guild Steps to Boston Common, Boston, MA; Municipal; Extant (I)

Museum of Fine Arts, Boston, MA; (job #73); Garden; Not extant

Tsuda University, Tokyo, Japan; (job #74); Academic; Master Plan (A)

William E. Atwood House, East Gloucester, MA; (job #415); Residence; Extant

Atwood Gallery-On-The-Moors, East Gloucester, MA; (job #416); Art Gallery; Extant (M)

1919

Ellingwood Funerary Chapel, Nahant, MA; (job #464); Ecclesiastical; Extant (R)

Sweet Briar College, Sweet Briar, VA; (job #610); Academic; Extant

The (Miss) Master's School, Dobbs Ferry, NY; (job #625); Academic; Status unknown

The (Miss) Master's School, Dobbs Ferry, NY; (job #626); Academic; Extant

The (Miss) Master's School, Dobbs Ferry, NY; (job #627); Academic; Status unknown

1920

Phillips Exeter Academy, Exeter, NH; Academic; Extant (A)

Trinity Episcopal Church, Houston, TX; (job #447); Ecclesiastical; Extant (R)

Library, Whitehall, Sudbury, MA; (job #448); Library; Extant

St. James Church for Angelica Gerry, Lake Delaware, NY; (job #461); Ecclesiastical; Extant (R)

Rosary College (Dominican University), River Forest, IL; (job #599); Academic (A)

Princeton University Chapel, Princeton, NJ; (job #600); Academic; Extant (A)

St. Stephen's Episcopal Church, Cohasset, MA; (job #616); Ecclesiastical; Extant

St. Francis House, Cambridge, MA; (job #618); Ecclesiastical; Extant

1921

Quincy High School, Quincy, MA; (job #594); Academic; Extant

Sacred Heart Church, Jersey City, NJ; (job #629); Ecclesiastical; Extant (R)

Roger Hayward House, Quincy, MA; (job #650); Residence

Lucius Beebe Memorial Library, Wakefield, MA; (job #695); Extant (M)

State Street United Church of Christ, Portland, ME; (job #743); Status unknown

National Life Insurance Company, Montpelier, VT; (job # 825); Office; Extant (M)

1922

Williams College, Williamstown, MA; Academic; Extant (A)

Princeton University, Princeton, NJ; Academic; Extant (A)

First Presbyterian Church, Utica, NY; (job #117); Ecclesiastical; Status unknown

Mercersburg Academy Chapel, Mercersburg, PA; (job #593); Ecclesiastical

Central Union Church, Honolulu, HI; (job #664); Ecclesiastical; Extant (R)

Second Presbyterian Church, Lexington, KY; (job #857); Ecclesiastical; Extant

1923

St. George's School Chapel, Newport, RI; (job #62); Ecclesiastical; Extant (R)

Williams College, Williamstown, MA; (job #75); Academic; Extant

First Presbyterian Church, Jamestown, NY; (job #119); Ecclesiastical; Unknown (R)

First Presbyterian Church, Tacoma, WA; (job #120); Ecclesiastical; Extant (R)

Agnes Scott College, Decatur, GA; (job #470); Academic

St. John's Episcopal Church Stained, Beverley Farms, MA; (job #631); Stained Glass; Extant

Evanston Lutheran Church, Evansville, IN; (job #649); Ecclesiastical; Status unknown

Quincy Women's Club, Quincy, MA; (job #651); Women's Club; Status unknown

Trinity Methodist Episcopal Church, Durham, NC; (job #738); Ecclesiastical; Extant (R)

State Street United Church of Christ, Portland, ME; (job #743A); Ecclesiastical; Status unknown

Choate School, Wallingford, CT; (job #1311);School Chapel; Extant (A)

1924

Blanche Sewall Residence, Houston, TX; (job #417); Residence; Extant (M)

Washington Cathedral, Washington, DC; (job #444); Ecclesiastical; Extant

St. Paul's Episcopal Church, Yonkers, NY; (job #591); Ecclesiastical; Status unknown (R)

Sweet Briar College, Sweet Briar, VA; (job #602); Academic; Extant (A)

Sweet Briar College, Sweet Briar, VA; (job #603); Academic; Extant

Church of the Resurrection, New York City, NY; (job #643); Ecclesiastical; Status unknown

National Presbyterian Church, Washington, DC; (job #648); Ecclesiastical; Not built (R)

St. Luke's Church, Norfolk, VA; (job #702); Ecclesiastical; Not built

Bryn Mawr College, Bryn Mawr, PA; (job #704); Academic; Master Plan

Wheaton College, Norton, MA; (job #712); Academic

1925

Sisters of St. Mary Home, Chicago, IL

Means House; (job #77); Residence; Extant

Society of Saint John the Evangelist, Cambridge, MA; (job #105); Ecclesiastical; Extant

Grace Cathedral, San Francisco, CA; (job #121); Ecclesiastical; Extant

Paul Watkins Residence, Winona, MN; (job #418); Residence; Extant (M)

Boston Architectural Club, Boston, MA; (job #437); Club; Extant

Woodrow Wilson Tomb / National, Washington, DC; (job #445); Memorial; Extant (M)

Choate School, Wallingford, CT; (job #462); Academic; Extant (A)

St. Mary's Catholic Church, Detroit, MI; (job #585); Ecclesiastical; Extant (R)

Cathedral of St. John the Divine, New York City, NY; (job #595); Ecclesiastical; Extant (I, R)

Greek Church of the Annunciation, Boston, MA; (job #688); Ecclesiastical; Status unknown

Williams College, Williamstown, MA; (job #742); Academic; Extant

1926

Houston Public Library, Houston, TX; Library; Extant **(I, M)**

Mercersburg Academy Chapel, Mercersburg, PA; (job #113); School Chapel; Extant

Angelica Livingston Gerry, Lake Delaware, NY; (job #419); Residence; Not Extant

Phillips Exeter Academy, Exeter, NH; (job #507); Academic; Extant **(M)**

Holy Cross Episcopal (Rosary), Pittsburgh, PA; (job #508); Ecclesiastical; Status unknown

American Military Cemetery, Belleau Wood, France; (job #509); Memorial; Extant **(M)**

American Military Cemetery, Oise Aisne, France; (job #510); Memorial; Extant **(M)**

Brown Memorial Presbyterian Church, Providence, RI; (job #511); Ecclesiastical; Status unknown

Virginia War Memorial Carillon, Richmond, VA; (job #512); Memorial; Extant **(M)**

Grace Lutheran Church, Malverne, NY; (job #513); Ecclesiastical; Unknown

American Military Cemetery, Belleau Wood, France; (job #575); Memorial; Extant **(M)**

1927

University of Notre Dame, South Bend, IN; (job #101); Academic; Extant **(A)**

Grace Evangelical Lutheran, Fremont, OH; (job #111); Ecclesiastical; Unknown

Church of St. Anne-In-The-Fields, Lincoln, MA; (job #134); Ecclesiastical; Not extant

St. Paul's School, Concord, NH; (job #514); School Chapel; Extant **(I, A)**

Christ Episcopal Church, Chattanooga, TN; (job #515); Ecclesiastical; Extant

Emmanuel Church, Rockford, IL; (job #516); Ecclesiastical; Not built **(R)**

American Church of Paris, Paris, France; (job #517); Ecclesiastical; Extant **(R)**

East Congregational Church, Grand Rapids, MI; (job #574); Ecclesiastical; Status unknown

St. Vincent's Church, Los Angeles, CA; (job #584); Ecclesiastical; Extant **(R)**

Sweet Briar College, Sweet Briar, VA; (job #604); Academic; Extant **(A)**

Sweet Briar College, Sweet Briar, VA; (job #611); Academic; Extant

Whitehall, Sudbury, MA; (job #628); Academic; Extant

St. Paul's Episcopal Church, Winston-Salem, NC; (job #641); Ecclesiastical; Extant **(R)**

Chapel at Bethany School for Girls, Glendale, OH; (job #642) School Chapel; Status unknown

Abbey Reformed United Church of Christ, Huntington, PA; (job #705); Ecclesiastical; Status unknown

1928

American Pro–Cathedral Church, Paris, France

St. Florian's Church, Detroit, MI; (job #110); Ecclesiastical; Extant **(R)**

Christ Church Cathedral Seal, St. Louis, MO; (job #518); Ecclesiastical; Status unknown

Hope Lutheran Church, Baltimore, MD; (job #519); Status unknown

Watkins Residence, Winona, MN; (job #521); Residence; Extant

Park Congregational Church, Grand Rapids, MI; (job #578); Status unknown

Cathedral of St. John's, Providence, RI; (job #588); Ecclesiastical; Extant

Sweet Briar College, Sweet Briar, VA; (job #606); Academic; Extant

Tyler House, North Andover, MA; (job #697); Residence; Extant

1929

Columbus Memorial Competition, Santo Domingo, DR; Memorial; Unsuccessful **(M)**

St. Albans School, Nat'l Cathedral, Washington, DC; (job #61); Academic; Extant **(A)**

Lucy Taggart–House of the Four, Gloucester, MA; (job #420); Residence; Status unknown

Church of St. John the Evangelist, St. Paul, MN; (job #438); Unknown; Status unknown

Prince Memorial Chapel, Fort Meyer, VA; (job #468); Ecclesiastical; Not built **(R)**

Wheaton College, Norton, MA; (job #520); Academic; Status unknown

St. John's Church, Watertown, CT; (job #522); Ecclesiastical; Status unknown

McCormack Federal Bldg., Boston MA; (job #523); Government; Extant (M)

First Methodist Episcopal Church, Evanston, IL; (job #524); Church; Status unknown

First Evangelical Lutheran Church, Louisville, KY; (job #525); Unknown; Status unknown

Klise Memorial Chapel, Grand Rapids, MI; (job #526); Ecclesiastical; Extant **(R)**

Church of St. Mary the Virgin, Falmouth Foreside, ME; (job #527); Ecclesiastical; Extant

St. Mary's Church, Burlington, NJ; (job #528); Ecclesiastical; Unknown

Swampscott High School, Swampscott, MA; (job #529); Academic; Master Plan

Phillips Exeter Academy, Exeter, NH; (job #530); Academic; Extant

Swampscott High School, Swampscott, MA; (job #531); Academic

Bishop Brent Memorial, Lausanne; (job #532); Memorial; Status unknown

Spring Lake Presbyterian Church, Spring Lake, NJ; (job #533); Ecclesiastical; Unknown

Christ Church–United Methodist, New York City, NY; (job #534); Ecclesiastical; Extant **(R)**

Phillips Exeter Academy, Exeter, NH; (job #535); Academic; Extant

Dexter Blvd Reform Church, Detroit, MI; (job #536); Ecclesiastical; Status unknown

Mass State House, Boston, MA; (job #538); State House; Not built

Bishop Seabury Memorial, Woodbury, CT; (job #537); Memorial; Status unknown

Reception House, Belleau Wood, France; (job #547); Reception House; Extant

Caretaker's House, Belleau Wood, France; (job #548); Residence; Extant

St. Andrew's Episcopal Church, Hopkinton, NH; (job #579); Ecclesiastical; Not built

Christ Church, Indianapolis, IN; (job #580); Ecclesiastical; Status unknown

Shepard House, Lenox, MA; (job #582); Residence; Status unknown

Princeton University, Princeton, NJ; (job #587); Academic; Extant **(A)**

St. John's Episcopal Church, Versailles, KY; (job #590); Unknown; Status unknown

St. Francis House (monastery), Cambridge, MA; (job #618A); Ecclesiastical; Extant

Grace Episcopal Church, Lawrence, MA; (job #665); Ecclesiastical; Extant

Gibson Chapel, Dyke-Green County, VA; (job #670); School Chapel; Extant **(R)**

All Saints Episcopal Church; Brookline, MA; (job #753A); Ecclesiastical; Extant **(R)**

1930

Scudder House, Bondville, VT; (job #425); Residence; Extant

St. Paul's Church, Akron, OH; (job #463); Ecclesiastical; Status unknown

Second Church of Christ Scientist, Hartford, CT; (job #472); Ecclesiastical; Status unknown

Independent Presbyterian Church, Savannah, GA; (job #476); Ecclesiastical; Status unknown

St. Paul's Church, Brooklyn, NY; (job #477); Ecclesiastical

Office Standards, Boston, MA; (job #539); Office

Evangelical Lutheran Church, St. Paul, MN; (job #540); Unknown; Status unknown

St. Mary's High & Grammar School, Glens Falls, NY; (job #541); Academic; Extant **(A)**

Phillips Exeter Academy, Exeter, NH; (job #542); Academic; Extant

Mount Calvary Episcopal Church, Baltimore, MD; (job #543); Unknown; Status unknown

Rice University, Houston, TX; (job #544); Academic; Extant

Standish Backus Residence, Detroit, MI; (job #545); Unknown; Status unknown

Phillips Exeter Academy, Exeter, NH; (job #546); Academic; Extant

Boston University, Boston, MA; (job #549); Academic; Master Plan

Harvard University, Cambridge, MA; (job #550); Academic; Extant (A)

St. James Church, Keene, NH; (job #551); Ecclesiastical; Status unknown

Phillips Exeter Academy, Exeter, NH; (job #552); Academic; Extant

Votive Chapel, Baltimore, MD; (job #555); Ecclesiastical; Status unknown

Phillips Exeter Academy, Exeter, NH; (job #557); Academic; Extant

Parker Hill Branch Library, Roxbury, MA; (job #559); Library; Extant (M)

St. Paul's Church, Brockton, MA; (job #560); Ecclesiastical; Not Extant

First (Old South) Church, Worcester, MA; (job #562); Ecclesiastical; Status unknown

South End Christian Church, Houston, TX; (job #563); Ecclesiastical; Status unknown

Phillips Exeter Academy, Exeter, NH; (job #564); Academic; Extant

Desloge Chapel, St Louis, MO; (job #565); Unknown; Status unknown

Wellesley College, Wellesley, MA; (job #566); Academic (A)

Chapel of the Annunciation, St Mary's County, MD; (job #567); Ecclesiastical; Status unknown

Fourth Presbyterian Church, Chicago, IL; (job #568); Church; Extant

Rollins College Chapel, Winter Park, FL; (job #569); School Chapel; Extant

St. Mark's Episcopal Church, Augusta, ME; (job #570); Ecclesiastical; Status unknown

Phillips Exeter Academy, Exeter, NH; (job #572); Academic; Extant

Mishawaka Cathedral, Mishawaka, IN; (job #573A); Ecclesiastical; Not built (R)

Belleau Wood (Aisne-Marne), Belleau Wood, France; (job #576); Reception; Extant

Belleau Wood (Aisne-Marne), Belleau Wood, France; (job #577); Caretaker Residence; Extant

University of Southern California, Los Angeles, CA; (job #583); Academic; Extant (I, A)

St. John's Episcopal Church, Savannah, GA; (job #589); Ecclesiastical; Status unknown

Sweet Briar College, Sweet Briar, VA; (job #605); Academic; Extant

Flather Memorial, Lowell, MA; (job #624); Memorial; Status unknown

Pymouth Quarries Inc., East Weymouth, MA; (job #652); Offices; Status unknown

St. George's Episcopal Church, Schenectady, NY; (job #653); Ecclesiastical; Status unknown

Office Standards, Boston, MA; (job #666); Office Standards; Extant

Church of St Edward the Martyr, Oklahoma City, OK; (job #689); School Chapel; Extant

Cathedral of St. John the Divine, New York City, NY, (job #737); Ecclesiastical; Extant

1931

Concordia Evangelical Lutheran, Louisville, KY; (job #439); Ecclesiastical; Extant

East Liberty Presbyterian Church, Pittsburgh, PA; (job #558); Ecclesiastical (R)

Church of Our Savior, Syracuse, NY; (job #460); Ecclesiastical; Extant

East Liberty Presbyterian Church, Pittsburgh, PA; (job #586); Garage; Extant

Phillips Exeter Academy, Exeter, NH; (job #596); Academic; Extant

Phillips Exeter Academy, Exeter, NH; (job #597); Academic; Extant

Phillips Exeter Academy, Exeter, NH; (job #598); Academic; Extant

St. Mark's Lutheran Church, Mauch Chunk, PA; (job #601); Ecclesiastical; Status unknown

Phillips Exeter Academy, Exeter, NH; (job #617); Academic; Extant

Cathedral of St. John the Divine, New York City, NY; (job #620); Ecclesiastical; Extant

St. Mary's Cathedral, Peoria, IL; (job #623); Renovation; Status unknown

Franklin Norse Memorial, Cambridge, MA; (job #633); Memorial; Status unknown

Copley Square Design, Boston, MA; (job #634); Square; Not built

Norwegian Lutheran Church, Roxbury, MA; (job #635); Ecclesiastical; Status unknown

Trinity Episcopal Chapel, Castine, ME; (job #637); Unknown; Status unknown

St. Mark's Pro–Cathedral-Hastings, NE; (job #638); Ecclesiastical; Unfinished

Cathedral of St. John the Divine, New York City. NY; (job #639); Ecclesiastical; Extant

St. Paul's School, Concord, NH; (job #640); School Project; Not built

Christ Episcopal Church, Quincy, MA; (job #645); Ecclesiastical; Status unknown

Williams College, Williamstown, MA; (job #646); Academic; Extant

Phillips Exeter Academy, Exeter, NH; (job #647); Academic; Extant

Church of the Holy Name, Swampscott, MA; (job #654); Ecclesiastical; Extant

Fenway War Memorial, Boston, MA; (job #655); Memorial; Status unknown

Harvard University, Cambridge, MA; (job #656); Restoration; Extant

St. James Episcopal Church, Delhi, NY; (job #658); Ecclesiastical; Extant

St. Peter's Church, Cambridge, MA; (job #659); unknown; Status unknown

Holy Trinity Episcopal Church, Tiverton, RI; (job #661); Ecclesiastical; Status unknown

Wheaton College, Norton, MA; (job #663); Academic; Not built (A)

Phillips Exeter Academy, Exeter, NH; (job #667); Academic; Extant (A)

Williams College, Williamstown, MA; (job #668); Academic; Extant

1932

Wellesley Play House, Wellesley, MA; (job #442); House; Extant

Phillips Exeter Academy, Exeter, NH; (job #556A); Academic; Extant

St. John's Episcopal Church Stained, Beverley Farms, MA; (job #631A); Ecclesiastical; Extant

Phillips Exeter Academy, Exeter, NH; (job #647A); Academic; Extant

Phillips Exeter Academy, Exeter, NH; (job #673); Academic; Extant (A)

Wheaton College, Norton, MA; (job #674); Academic; Not built

First Church of Christ, Sharon, CT; (job #676); Ecclesiastical; Status unknown

Gavit Headstone (Ms. Julia Gavit), Sharon, CT; (job #677); Memorial; Status unknown

Wheaton College, Norton, MA; (job #679); Academic; Extant (I)

Wheaton College, Norton, MA; (job #680); Academic

St. Paul's Episcopal Cathedral, Detroit, MI; (job #681); Ecclesiastical; Extant

Phillips Exeter Academy, Exeter, NH; (job #683); Academic; Extant

Phillips Exeter Academy, Exeter, NH; (job #683A); Academic; Extant

Hyde Park Branch Library, Hyde Park, MA; (job #685); Library; Status unknown

Wheaton College, Norton, MA; (job #686); Academic; Extant

University of California, Pasadena, CA; (job #687); Status unknown

All Saints Church, Worcester, MA; (job #715); Ecclesiastical; Extant

1933

Bourne & Sagamore Bridges, Bourne, MA; (job #703); Bridge; Extant **(M)**

Stedman Traveling Altar, Jamaica Plain, MA; (job #692); Ecclesiastical; Status unknown

Christ Church, Cambridge, MA; (job #694); Ecclesiastical; Not Applicable

St. Stephen's Episcopal Church, Providence, RI; (job #698); Renovations; Not built

Cathedral of St. John the Divine, New York City, NY; (job #699); Ecclesiastical; Extant

Phillips Church, Exeter, NH; (job #700); Ecclesiastical; Not built

Church of the Holy Innocents, West Orange, NJ; (job #701); Ecclesiastical; Status unknown

Bryn Mawr College, Bryn Mawr, PA; (job #704A); Academic; Master Plan

Bryn Mawr College, Bryn Mawr, PA; (job #704B); Academic; Not built

Bryn Mawr College, Bryn Mawr, PA; (job #704C); Academic; Not built

Wheaton College, Norton, MA; (job #706A); Academic; Extant

Wheaton College, Norton, MA; (job #707A); Academic; Extant

St. Bernard's Episcopal Church, Bernardsville, NJ; (job #708); Ecclesiastical; Status unknown

1934

Phillips Exeter Academy, Exeter, NH; (job #713); Academic; Extant

Phillips Exeter Academy, Exeter, NH; (job #714); Academic; Extant

Hingham Junior High School, Hingham, MA; (job #716); Academic; Extant

Garden House, Clinton, NY; (job #717); Residence

St. James Episcopal Church, New York City, NY; (job #718); Ecclesiastical; Extant

St. James Episcopal Church, New York City, NY; (job #719); Ecclesiastical; Extant

FU Chapel, Gainesville, FL; (job #720); Academic; Not built

Holy Cross Monastery Campanile, West Park, NY; (job #721); Ecclesiastical; Extant **(M)**

Williams College, Williamstown, MA; (job #722); Academic; Extant

St. John's Church, Detroit, MI; (job #725); Ecclesiastical; Status unknown

Wheaton College, Norton, MA; (job #726); Academic; Extant

Christ Church, Montpelier, VT; (job #727); Ecclesiastical; Status unknown

Shimmo House for A.E. Hoyle, Nantucket, MA; (job #729); Residence; Extant

Phillips Exeter Academy, Exeter, NH; (job #728); Academic; Extant

Cora Harris Chapel, Rydal, GA; (job #730); Ecclesiastical; Extant

Wheaton College, Norton, MA; (job #731); Academic; Extant

Second Church Unitarian, Boston, MA; (job #732); Ecclesiastical; Extant **(R)**

1935

George Washington Memorial, Washington, DC; (job #733); Memorial; Not built

Oak Grove Cemetery, Falmouth, MA; (job #734); Ecclesiastical; Extant

William B. Rice Eventide Home. Quincy, MA; (job #735); Residence; Status unknown

Norfolk County Hospital, Braintree, MA; (job #736); Hospital; Extant

Swampscott High School. Swampscott, MA; (job #739); Academic; Proposal

Hampton Harbor Yacht Club, Hampton, NH; (job #740); Yacht Club; Status unknown

Williams College, Williamstown, MA; (job #744); Academic; Status unknown

Trinity Episcopal Church, Haverhill, MA; (job #745); Ecclesiastical; Extant

Swarthmore College, Swarthmore, PA; (job #746); Academic; Master Plan

Swarthmore College, Swarthmore, PA; (job #746A); Academic; Not built **(A)**

Swarthmore College, Swarthmore, PA; (job #746B); Academic; Not built **(A)**

Swarthmore College, Swarthmore, PA; (job #746C); Academic; Not built

Swarthmore College, Swarthmore, PA; (job #746D); Academic; Not built

Swarthmore College, Swarthmore, PA; (job #746E); Academic; Not built

Retreat House & Bishop Memorial Pulpit, Burlington, VT; (job #747); Retreat House; Status unknown

St. Thomas Episcopal Church, Dover, NH; (job #748); Ecclesiastical; Status unknown

Webster University Library, St. Louis, MO; (job #749); Library; Not built

St. Paul's School, Concord, NH; (job #750); Library; Extant

St. Mark's Evangelical Church, New Albany, IN; (job #751); Ecclesiastical; Status unknown

Blank Church, Chicago, IL; (job #752); Ecclesiastical; Not built **(R)**

Waterfront Development, Portsmouth, NH; (job #753); Development; Extant **(M)**

Church of Our Savior, Brookline, MA; (job #755); Ecclesiastical; Extant

Nurse's Home, Braintree, MA; (job #756); Residence; Status unknown

All Saints Episcopal Church, Chelmsford, MA; (job #757); Ecclesiastical; Status unknown

Wheaton College, Norton, MA; (job #758): Academic: Extant

Quincy Court House, Quincy, MA; (job #759); Courthouse; Extant

St. Paul's Cathedral, Detroit, MI; (job #760); Ecclesiastical; Extant

First Congregational Church, Concord, NH; (job #761); Ecclesiastical; Status unknown

St. Paul's Episcopal Cathedral, Detroit, MI; (job #762); Ecclesiastical; Extant

Church of St. John the Evangelist, Cambridge, MA; (job #764) Ecclesiastical

Church of St. John the Evangelist, Cambridge, MA; (job #765); Ecclesiastical; Extant

St. Mark's School, Southborough, MA; (job #766); Academic; Not built

Cathedral of St. John the Divine, New York City, NY; (job # 816); Ecclesiastical; Not built

1936

Calvary Episcopal Church, Americus, GA; (job #123); Ecclesiastical; Extant

Conventual Church of St. Mary &, Cambridge, MA; (job #754); Ecclesiastical; Extant **(R)**

Blank House, Chicago, IL; (job #767); Residence; Status unknown

Phillips Exeter Academy, Exeter, NH; (job #768); Academic; Extant

Provident Mutual Life Ins. Co., Philadelphia, PA, (job #769); Office; Extant

Williams College, Williamstown, MA; (job #770); Academic; Extant

All Saints Church, Tupelo, MI: (job #771); Ecclesiastical: Not built

First Presbyterian Church–Church of the Covenant, Washington, DC; (job #772); Ecclesiastical; Status unknown

St. Paul's Cathedral, Detroit, MI; (job #773); Ecclesiastical; Status unknown

St. Peter's Church, Jamaica Plain, MA; (job #774); Ecclesiastical; Status unknown

Stockbridge Public Library, Stockbridge, MA; (job #775); Library Additions; Extant

St. Paul's School, Concord, NH; (job #776); Academic; Status unknown

First Congregational Church, Westfield, MA; (job #777); Ecclesiastical; Status unknown

St. Andrew's Episcopal Church, Astoria, NY; (job #778); Ecclesiastical; Status unknown

Church of the Holy Name, Swampscott, MA; (job #779); Ecclesiastical

Scudder Residence, Bondville, VT; (job #780); Residence; Extant

Phillips Exeter Academy, Exeter, NH; (job #781); Academic; Extant

Central Baptist Church, Providence, RI; (job #782); Ecclesiastical; Status unknown

House for Deerfield Academy, Deerfield, MA; (job #783); Academic

St. James Church, Pennington, GA; (job #784); Ecclesiastical; Status unknown

Proposed Church, Wichita, KS; (job #785); Ecclesiastical; Status unknown

Trinity Cathedral, Phoenix, AZ; (job #786); Ecclesiastical; Status unknown

Mrs. William Craig House, Pinehurst, MD; (job #787); Residence; Status unknown

Lutheran Church, Berkeley, CA; (job #788); Ecclesiastical; Status unknown

Grace Episcopal Church, Utica, NY; (job #789); Ecclesiastical; Status unknown

Bethany Congregational Church, Montpelier, VT; (job #790); Ecclesiastical; Status unknown

Convention Recreation Center, Hull, MA; (job #791); Recreation Ctr.

Sweet Briar College, Sweet Briar, VA; (job #792); Academic; Not built (A)

1937

Caproni Monument, Roxbury, MA; (job #793); Monument

Norfolk County District Courthouse, Dedham, MA; (job #795); Courthouse; Extant (M)

Phillips Exeter Academy, Exeter, NH; (job #796); Academic; Extant

Wood Art Gallery, Montpelier, VT; (job #797); Gallery; Status unknown

St. Paul's School, Concord, NH; (job #798); Academic; Extant

Jelke Residence, Newport, RI; (job #799); Residence; Status unknown

Trinity Church, Boston, MA; (job #800); Ecclesiastical; Status unknown

Gillett Mausoleum, Westfield, MA; (job #801); Mausoleum; Status unknown

St. James Episcopal Church, Woonsocket, RI; (job #802); Ecclesiastical; Status unknown

Epiphany Episcopal Church, Providence, RI; (job #804); Ecclesiastical; Not Extant

St. Stephen's Church, Portland, ME; (job #805); Ecclesiastical

Trinity Episcopal Church, St. Augustine, FL; (job #806); Ecclesiastical; Status unknown

Purinton House, Stockbridge, MA; (job #807); Residence

Independent Congregational, Battle Creek, MI; (job #808); Unknown; Status unknown

Huguenot United Methodist Church, Richmond, VA; (job #809); Ecclesiastical; Status unknown

St. Agnes School, Albany, NY; (job #810); Academic; Status unknown

Mission Church Order of the Holy, Liberia; (job #811); Ecclesiastical; Status unknown

Princeton University, Princeton, NJ; (job #812); Academic; Extant

Quincy Trade School-Section H.S., Quincy, MA; (job #813); Academic

1938

Bourne Bridge, Bourne, MA: Municipal; Extant (M)

Sagamore Bridge, Sagamore, MA; Municipal; Extant (M)

St. Andrew's Memorial Episcopal, Detroit, MI; (job #43); Ecclesiastical; Burned

New England Mutual Life Insurance, Boston, MA; (job #814); Office; Extant (M)

Greenville Congregational Church, Norwich, CT; (job #815); Ecclesiastical; Status unknown

First Presbyterian Church, Greensburg, PA; (job #818); Ecclesiastical; Extant

St. Stephen's Church of the Martyr, Minneapolis, MN; (job #819); Unknown; Status unknown

All Saints Episcopal Church, Winter Park, FL; (job #820); Ecclesiastical; Extant (R)

Samuel Smith Drury, Concord, NH; (job #821); Unknown; Status unknown

Church of St. Raphael the Archangel, Oakland, CA; (job #822); Ecclesiastical; Status unknown

Community Centre, Morrisville, VT; (job #824); Community; Status unknown

Rollins College, Winter Park, FL; (job #826); Academic; Extant

Congregational Church, Woodstock, CA; (job #827); Ecclesiastical; Status unknown

Williams College, Williamstown, MA; (job #828); Academic; Extant

Williams College, Williamstown, MA; (job #829); Academic; Extant (A)

St. Andrew's Church, Detroit, MI; (job #830); Unknown; Status unknown

Countryside School, Newton Highlands, MA; (job #1038); Academic; Status unknown

1939

Church of the Advent, Boston, MA; (job #823); Furnishings; Extant

Hampton Academy, Hampton, NH; (job #831); Academic; Extant

St. Paul's Episcopal Church, Concord, NH; (job #832); Ecclesiastical; Status unknown

Zion Lutheran Church, Ambridge, PA; (job #833); Ecclesiastical; Status unknown

St. Stephen's Church, Fort Yukon, AS; (job #834); Ecclesiastical; Not built

Christ–Frederica Episcopal Church, St. Simon's Island, GA; (job #835); Ecclesiastical; Status unknown

Culver Military Academy, Culver, IN; (job #836); School Chapel; Extant

St. Thomas Church, Peoria, IL; (job #837); Ecclesiastical; Status unknown (R)

St. Phillip's Episcopal Church, Charleston, SC; (job #838); Memorial; Extant

Most Rev. J.H. Schlarman, Peoria, IL; (job #839); Residence; Status unknown

Harry McAllister Residence, Rochelle, GA; (job #840); Residence; Status unknown

United Congregational Church, Hampton, NH; (job #841); Ecclesiastical; Status unknown

St. Paul's Church, Dayton, OH; (job #842); Ecclesiastical; Status unknown

Out-Door Altar, Bishop, WY; (job #843); Ecclesiastical; Status unknown

Grace Episcopal Church, Newark, NJ; (job #844); Ecclesiastical

St. Luke's Episcopal Church, Mechanicsville, NY; (job #845); Ecclesiastical; Status unknown

First & Franklin Street Presbyterian, Baltimore, MD; (job #846); Ecclesiastical; Status unknown

Boston University, Boston, MA; (job #847): Academic; Master Plan

Charles M. Dale Office Building, Portsmouth, NH; (job #848); Office; Not built

Grace Episcopal Church, Medford, MA; (job #849); Ecclesiastical; Status unknown

North America Physical Fitness, Boston, MA; (job #850); Office

Grace Episcopal Church, Medford, MA; (job #851); Ecclesiastical; Status unknown

Grosse Pointe Unitarian Church, Grosse Pointe, MI; (job #852); Unknown; Not built

Memorial to Arthur Page Brown, San Francisco, CA; (job #853); Memorial; Status unknown

Roberts' House, Portsmouth, NH; (job #854); Restoration; Status unknown

Rice University, Houston, TX; (job #855); Academic; Status unknown

House Corner Mercy St. & Manning, Portsmouth, NH; (job #856); Restoration; Extant

St. Paul's Church, Pawtucket, RI; (job #858); Ecclesiastical; Extant

First United Methodist Church, North Andover, MA; (job #859); Ecclesiastical; Not built

Fort Devens, Ayer, MA; (job #860); Military

Prudential Tower, Boston, MA; (job #860A); Office; Not built

Charles M. Dale Residence, North Hampton, NH; (job #861); Residence; Status unknown

Marcy Street Apartments, Portsmouth, NH; (job #862); Residence; Status unknown

Society for the Prevention of Cruelty, Northampton, NH; (job #863); Office; Status unknown

McCormick Presbyterian, Chicago, IL; (job #864); Academic; Status unknown

1941

US. Army–Motor Repair Shop; (job #865); Military

Society of St. John the Evangelist, Boston, MA; (job #866A); Ecclesiastical

East Liberty Presbyterian Church, Pittsburgh, PA; (job #866); Ecclesiastical; Extant

U.S. Military Academy, West Point, NY; (job #867); Competition; Unsuccessful

Cutter Langdon House, Portsmouth, NH; (job #868); Residence; Status unknown

First Presbyterian Church, Lincoln, NE; (job #869); Ecclesiastical; Status unknown

U.S. Foundation for War Research; (job #870); Military

USA Project–Concrete Tower, Long Island, NY; (job #871); Military; Status unknown

1942

Merchants National Bank, Boston, MA; (job #122); Office Interior; Not Extant

USA Project-Concrete Tower-Bailey's Island, Portland Harbor, ME; (job #872); Military; Status unknown

Church–Rt. Rev. W. K. Mitchell, Phoenix, AZ; (job#873); Ecclesiastical; Status unknown

Portsmouth Defense Area Loc, Hampton, NH; (job #874); Military; Status unknown

Portsmouth Defense Area Loc, Rye, NY; (job #874A); Military; Status unknown

Federal Housing Authority, So. Portland, ME; (job #875); Residences; Status unknown

Boston Harbor Defense Area, Boston, MA; (job #876); Defense; Status unknown

Cathedral of St. John the Divine, New York City, NY; (job #877); Ecclesiastical; Extant

Seabury–Western Seminary Chapel, Evanston, IL; (job #878); Ecclesiastical; Status unknown

Rental Space at 92 Newbury St., Boston, MA; (job #1039); Office Interior; Demolished

1943

St. Michael's Episcopal Church, Milton, MA; (job #135); Ecclesiastical; Extant

Boston University, Boston, MA; (job #880); Academic; Extant

First Congregational Church, Milton, MA; (job #886); Ecclesiastical; Extant

Wollaston Federal Savings & Loan, Wollaston, MA; (job #887); Bank; Extant

Worcester St. Railway Company, Worcester, MA; (job #888); Office; Extant

Norfolk County Registry, Dedham, MA; (job #884); Office; Extant

Raymond Monument–Forest Hill, Boston, MA; (job #883); Monument; Extant

Bradford Junior College, Haverhill, MA; (job #881); Academic; Extant

Harbor Defense-Fletcher Neck Tower, Portland, ME; (job #879); Defense Tower; Extant

Cathedral of St. John the Divine, New York City, NY; (job #885); Ecclesiastical; Not built

St. Mary's Catholic Church, Glens Falls, NY; (job #889), Ecclesiastical; Extant

Lady Chapel, New York City, NY; (job #890); Ecclesiastical; Extant

Church Mission House, New York City, NY; (job #882); Ecclesiastical; Extant

Bibliography

All Saints Parish Church. *The Stained Glass of All Saints*. Peterborough, NH: All Saint's Parish Church, 2001.

Allen, George H. "Cram—The Yankee Mediaevalist." *The Architectural Forum* (July 1931): 79–80.

Amero, Richard. "History of California Building in Balboa Park." *San Diego Historical Society*. http://www.synergyicons.com/pac/ac/camuseum/history/History.htm (Accessed October 2006)

Architectural Record (January 1911): 1106.

Avery, Ralph Emmett. *America's triumph at Panama*. Chicago: The L.W. Walter Co., 1913.

Badger, Richard, ed. *Calvary Church, Pittsburgh, Pennsylvania*. Boston: The Gorham Press, 1908.

Baker, James McFarlan. *American Churches, Volume II*. New York: The American Architect, 1915.

Brighton, Ray. *The Prescott Story*. New Castle, New Hampshire: The Portsmouth Marine Society, 1982.

Brown, Chester Anderson. *My Best Years in Architecture with Ralph Adams Cram, FAIA*. Unpublished. Manuscript, 1971.

Burianek, Bridget. *Ralph Adams Cram and Concordia Lutheran Church of Lousiville, Kentucky*. http://www.concordia-lutheran.com/archhist.htm (Accessed October 2006)

Calvary Episcopal Church. *A Guide to Calvary Episcopal Church*. Pittsburgh: Calvary Episcopal Church,1980.

Caswell, Harold. "The Graduate College of Princeton University." *American Architect*, vol. C, no. 1870 (October 25, 1911): 165–171.

Catholic Encyclopedia. *Gothic Architecture*. http://www.knight.org/advent/cathen/066656.htm (Accessed October 2006)

Conn, Stetson. *The Episcopal Church in Winter Park 1883–1983*. Winter Park, Florida: All Saints Episcopal Church, 1984.

Cosper, Kathryn Perrin. *Covenant Presbyterian Church: The First Fifty Years*. Charlotte, North Carolina: Covenant Presbyterian Church, 1997.

Cram, Ralph Adams. *A Plan for the Settlement of Middle Europe on the Principle of Partition without Annexation*, 1918. In *American Gothic: The Mind and Art of Ralph Adams Cram*, by Robert Muccigrosso. Washington, D.C.: University Press of America, 1980.

———. "Spanish Notes." *American Architect* CXXV, no. 2437 (January 1924): 47–53.

———. "A Note on Bryn Athyn Church." *The American Architect* (n.d.): 710–713.

———. *American Churches, vol. I*. New York: The Architectural Book Publishing Company, 1915.

———. *American Church Building of Today*. New York: The Architectural Book Publishing Company, Inc., 1929.

———. *Church Building*. 3rd ed. Boston: Small, Maynard & Company, 1914.

———. *Contemporary American Architects*. New York and London: Whittlesey House, McGraw-Hill Book Company, Inc., 1931.

———. *Convictions and Controversies*. (Essay Index Reprint Series). Freeport, New York: Books for Libraries Press, 1970.

———. "Decadence of French Church Architecture." *The Architectural Forum* (March 1929): 305–309.

———. *English Country Churches*. Boston: Bates & Co, 1898.

———. *Farm Houses, Manor Houses, Minor Chateaux and Small Churches from the Sixteenth Centuries in Normandy, Brittany and Other Parts of France*. New York: The Architectural Book Publishing Company/Paul Wenzel and Maurice Krakow, 1917.

———. *My Life in Architecture*. Boston: Little, Brown, and Company, 1936.

———. *The End of Democracy*. Boston: Marshall Jones Company, 1937.

———. *The Gothic Quest*. New York: The Baker and Taylor Company, 1907.

———. *The Ministry of Art*. Boston and New York: Houghton Mifflin Company, 1914.

———. *The Nemesis of Mediocrity*. Boston: Marshall Jones Company, 1917.

———. *The Ruined Abbeys of Great Britain*. New York: James Pott & Company, 1905.

———. "Some Architectural and Spiritual Aspects of the Chapel: The Challenge Offered by Princeton's New Edifice, and the Answer Which the Future Can Give It." *The Princeton Alumni Weekly* (May 25, 1928): 987–989, 1028.

———. *The Substance of Gothic: Six Lectures on the Development of Architecture from Charlemagne to Henry VIII*. 2nd ed. Boston: Marshall Jones Company, 1925.

———. "The Test of Beauty." *Harvard Graduate's Magazine*, vol. XXX, no. CXVII (September 1921): 1–20.

———. *Towards the Great Peace*. Boston: Marshall Jones Company, 1922.

———. *Walled Towns*. Boston: Marshall Jones Company, 1919.

Cram, William Everett Cram. *Time and Change*. Boston: Marshall Jones Company, 1927.

Davis-Cooley, Gayle. *Pillar of Faith: Trinity Church at 100*. Houston, Texas: Trinity Episcopal Church, 1992.

Design Graphics World. "Great Architectural Drawings Displayed at Museum." (March 1985): 42–43.

DiMauro, Laurie, ed. *Twentieth-Century Literary Criticism*, vol. 45. Detroit: Gale Research, Inc., 1992.

Doll, John G. *Heart of the Hilltop: The St. George's School Chapel*. Newport, Rhode Island: St. George's School, 2003.

The East Presbyterian Church. Pittsburgh: The East Liberty Pittsburgh Church, 1935.

The Exeter Bulletin. "The Father of Phillips Church." (Spring, 2003).

Fletcher, Herbert H. *A History of The Church of Our Saviour*. Brookline, Massachusetts: The Parish Council of the Church, 1936.

Gardner, John H. *The First Presbyterian Church of Baltimore: Two Century Chronicle*. Baltimore:The First Presbyterian Church, 1962.

Glenn, Bruce E. *Bryn Athyn Cathedral: The Building of a Church*. New York: C. Harrison Conroy Co., Inc., 1971.

Grant, Tina and Joann Cerrito, eds. *Modern Arts Criticism*, vol. 3, *Ralph Adams Cram*. Detroit: Gale Research Inc., 1993.

Hammond, Mason. "The Enclosure of the Harvard Yard." *Harvard Library Bulletin* (Fall 1983).

Hitchcock, Henry-Russell. "Architecture: Nineteenth and Twentieth Centuries." In *The Pelican History of Art*, edited by Nikolaus Pevsner. New York: Penguin Books, 1978.

Inskip, Peter. *Edwin Lutyens*. In Architectural Monographs Series, No. 6, edited by Robert A. M Stern. London: Academy Editions, 1986. New York: St. Martin's Press, 1986.

Johnson, Wilbur E. *The New Home of the Provident Mutual Life*

Insurance Company. Philadelphia: Provident Mutual Life Insurance Company, 1928.

Kelly, Rev. Joseph P. Kelly. *The History of Mary's Parish, Glens Falls, New York, 1848–1949*. Glens Falls, New York: Glens Falls Post Company, 1949.

Kelsey, Albert ed. *The Christopher Columbus Memorial Lighthouse Competition*. Issued by the Pan-American Union, 1930.

Kilham Jr., Walter H. *Raymond Hood, Architect: Form Through Function in the American Skyscraper*. New York: Architectural Book Publishing Co., Inc., 1973.

Kock, Robert L. *Louis C. Tiffany, Rebel in Glass*. New York: Crown Publishers, Inc., 1982.

L.A. Architect. "L.A./AIA Honors Lunden." (December 1983): 1.

Lee, William C. *Reaching Out: The First 150 Years of Trinity English Lutheran Church*. Fort Wayne, Indiana: Trinity English Lutheran Church, 1996.

Loring, Bronwyn Evans. *St. John's Stained Glass*. Beverly Farms, Massachusetts: St. John's Episcopal Church, 1985.

Loring, Charles G. "The Boston Federal Building." *American Architect* (November 1933): 15–19.

Lunden, Samuel E. "The Arts and Architecture of the Edward L. Doheny, Jr. Memorial Library." Los Angeles, 1983.http://www.publicartinla.com/USCArt/Doheny/semicentennial.html

Macrae-Gibson, Gavin. "Reflections Upon the New Beginnings at The Cathedral of Saint John the Divine." *Architectural Record* (November 1979): 119–126.

McKean, Hugh F. *The "Lost" Treasures of Louis Comfort Tiffany*. New York: Double Day & Company, Inc., 1980.

Moore, Charles. *Daniel H. Burnham: Architect Planner of Cities*, Vol. 1, 126. Boston: Houghton Mifflin Co., 1921. In *American Gothic: The Mind and Art of Ralph Adams Cram*, by Robert Muccigrosso. Washington, D.C.: University Press of America, 1980, 81.

Morgan, William. *The Almighty Wall: The Architecture of Henry Vaughan*. In American Monograph Series, edited by Robert A. M. Stern. New York: The Architectural History Foundation, 1983. Cambridge, Massachusetts and London: The MIT Press, 1983.

Muccigrosso, Robert. *American Gothic: The Mind and Art of Ralph Adams Cram*. Washington, D.C.: University Press of America, 1980.

Newburyport Daily News. "Hampton Falls to Celebrate," August 15, 1922.

Newburyport Daily News. "Hampton Falls is 200 yrs Old," August 25, 1922.

Nichols, W. A. "Fourth Presbyterian Church of Chicago." *The Architectural Record* XXXVI, no. 3 (September 1914): 4, 178–199.

Nichols, Ann. "Exemplary Gothic Style." *Chattanooga Free Press*, December 26, 1993.

Nicholson, Patrick J. *William Ward Watkin and the Rice Institute*. Houston, Texas: Gulf Publishing Company, 1991.

Norfleet, Elizabeth Copeland. *Blue Ridge School: Samaritans of the Mountains*. Orange,Virginia: Green Publishers, Inc., 1982.

Oliver, Richard. *Bertram Grosvenor Goodhue*. In American Monograph Series, edited by Robert A.M. Stern. New York: The Architectural History Foundation, 1983. Cambridge, Massachusetts and London: The MIT Press, 1983.

————. "Voyages of the Imagination: Four Post-Modern Buildings of Bertram Goodhue." *Architectural Record* (September 1978): 101–108.

Perry, Marguerite C., ed. *Grace Church 1848–1948*. Medford, Massachusetts: Grace Church, 1948.

Pratt, Joan C. "Ralph Adams Cram and the Gothic Quest: From Phillips Church, Exeter to St. John the Divine, New York." *The Exeter Bulletin* (Spring 1983): 5–10.

Price, Matlack. "The Chapel at St. George's School, Newport." *The Architectural Forum*, (May 1929): 661–678.

Ruskin, John. *Mornings in Florence*. London: George Allen, 1904.

Sanders, Rev. Robert Stuart. *History of the Second Presbyterian Church, Lexington, Kentucky: Of the United Presbyterian Church in the USA, 1815–1965*. Lexington, Kentucky: Second Presbyterian Church, 1965.

Schuyler, Montgomery. "The Work of Cram, Goodhue & Ferguson." *The Architectural Record* XXIX (January 1911): 87.

Seckinger, Ernie. *American Transcendentalism Thoughts and Links*. http://www.zebra.net/~ernie. Seckinger/transcendentalism.htm

Shand-Tucci, Douglass. *Boston Bohemia 1881–1900, vol. I Ralph Adams Cram: Life and Architecture*. Amherst, Massachusetts: University of Massachusetts Press, 1995.

————. *Built in Boston: City and Suburb 1800–1950*. New York: New York Graphic Society, 1978.

Simonson, Mark. "Politics to Philanthropy." *The Daily Star Online*, January 18, 2003. http://www.theDailystar.com/opinion/columns/simonson/2003/01simonson0118.htm

Simpson, Duncan. *C. F .A. Voysey, an architect of individuality*. London: Lund Humphries, 1979.

Skinner, Orin E., ed., *Stained Glass* XXXVII, no. IV (Winter 1942).

Spofford, William B. "The New St. Paul's , Winston Salem." *The Witness* XIV, no. 21, (Jan. 2, 1930): 2.

Summerson, John, David Watkin, and G. Tilman Mellinghoff. *John Soane. In Architectural Monographs Series*, No. 8, edited by Robert A. M. Stern. London: Academy Editions, 1983. New York: St. Martin's Press, 1983.

Tardiff, Olive. "Cram: Genius or Eccentric?" *The Exeter Newsletter*, July 21, 1982.

Tenner, Edward. "Yankee Feudalist: Collegiate Gothic Architect Ralph Adams Cram." *Princeton Alumni Weekly*, January 15, 1986, 15–17.

Tilly, Maureen A. *The Sign Value of Donatist Baptismal Architecture or Baptisteries Rebaptized*. http://Divinity.library.vanderbilt.edu/burns/chroma/baptism/tillbapt.html

Time Magazine. "Christian Architect." October 5, 1942. http://time.com/time/archive/preview/0.10987.773756.00.html

————. "Protestantism is Bankrupt." January 6, 1936. http://www.time.com/time/archive/preview/0.1098775557900.html

————. "Skyward." December 13, 1926. http://www.time.com/time/magazine/article/subscriber/0.100987.722883.00.html

The Trustees of the Hunt Building. *Images of America: Nashua In Time and Place*. Charleston, South Carolina: Arcadia Publishing, 1999.

Warneck, Stephen. *Ralph Adams Cram: The Man, His Work, and His Legacy at Princeton University*. http://mondrian.princeton.edu/CampusWWW/Studentdocs/Cram.html

Waterhouse, Margaret Thom, ed. *The Story of St. Paul's: 1956–1959*. Chicago: St. Paul's Protestant Episcopal Church, 1959.

Watkin, David. *English Architecture: A Concise History*. New York and Toronto: Oxford University Press, 1979.

Watts, Lisa. "The Masque of Power: The Ultimate Housewarming Party." *Technology Review*, (July 1991): 6–8.

Whitaker, Charles Harris, ed. *Bertram Grosvenor Goodhue—Architect and Master of Many Arts*. New York: Press of the American Institute of Architects, Inc., 1925, Plates XIX, XXXIV, LXXVIII.

White, Theo B. *Paul Philippe Cret: Architect and Teacher*. Philadelphia: The Art Alliance Press, 1973.

Whitehill, Walter Muir. *Boston: A Topographical History*. 2nd ed. Cambridge, Massachusetts: The Belknap Press of Harvard University Press. 1968.

Whitehill, Walter Muir and Frederick Doveton Nichols. *Palladio in America*. New York: Rizzoli International Publications, Inc., 1978.

Wuonola, Mark A. *Church of the Advent, Boston: A Guidebook*. Boston: The Parish of the Advent, 1975.

Van Leeuwen, Thomas A.P. *The Skyward Trend of Thought*. The Hague: AHA Books, 1986.

Index